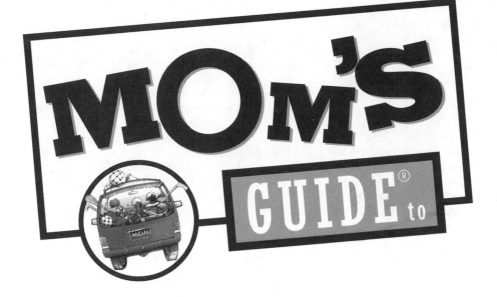

Sports

VICKI PORETTA
& DEB CRISFIELD

alpha
books

A Division of Macmillan General Reference
A Simon & Schuster Macmillan Company
1633 Broadway, New York, NY 10019-6785

Macmillan Publishing books may be purchased for business or sales promotional use. For information please write: Special Markets Department, Macmillan Publishing USA, 1633 Broadway, New York, NY 10019-6785.

International Standard Book Number: 0-02-861966-8

Library of Congress Catalog Card Number: 97-073184

99 98 97   4 3 2 1

Interpretation of the printing code: The rightmost number of the first series of numbers is the year of the book's printing; the rightmost number of the second series of numbers is the number of the book's printing. For example, a printing code of 97-1 shows that the first printing occurred in 1997.

Printed in the United States of America

Alpha Development Team

Brand Manager: Kathy Nebenhaus
Executive Editor: Gary M. Krebs
Managing Editor: Bob Shuman
Senior Editor: Nancy Mikhail
Development Editor: Jennifer Perillo
Editorial Assistant: Maureen Horn

Production Team

Director of Editorial Services: Brian Phair
Production Editor: Phil Kitchel
Copy Editor: Lisa Lord
Illustrator: George McKeown
Designer: George McKeown
Indexer: Chris Barrick
Production Team: Daniela Raderstorf, Laure Robinson, Maureen West

Look for these additional titles in the Mom's Guides® series...

Contents

Introduction

It's over. You took the plunge into the Sports Mom Whirlpool. Your son signed up for the town's Little League program, and he's already won his first game. You try to relive the glory with him, but you thought "strike" meant "to hit," and now you're both confused. Don't worry. Help is on the way. This book was written with muddled moms in mind.

The *Mom's Guide to Sports* covers 10 popular kids' sports in detail. All the rules are explained—especially the confusing ones. Offsides? Icing? The infield fly rule? Ever have any trouble with these? This book is the answer. Positions are explained, so you don't have to nod vaguely when your daughter says she's a swing hitter on her volleyball team. Moves, scoring, and ref signals are explained in many chapters, and almost all of them include games you can play at home. Finally, in each chapter there's a vocabulary list so you can talk sports with the best of them.

But sports aren't just a matter of rules and referees. Many parents are concerned about the levels of competition, the potential for injuries, and the financial costs of playing a sport. Choosing the right sport for your child can be difficult. And while coaches are usually wonderful volunteers who love kids and sports, you may end up with one who is a bad match for your child. Town and school programs differ in quality, too. This book tells you what to look for in all of these arenas.

Finally, the book ends with a chapter on how to be the ultimate Sports Mom. Tips on nutrition, ego boosting, and fan behavior are covered. With a little help, your child's sports experience can be fun for everyone in your family.

EXTRAS

In addition to giving you detailed explanations for each sport, this book also provides you with some extra information, either an anecdote that might clarify a rule or a tidbit that's not necessarily crucial, but might just be fun. Look for these boxes throughout the book:

INSTANT REPLAY

These are strange but true stories that have happened to veteran Sports Moms and kids. Believe them or not, but take them to heart.

TAKING A CLOSER LOOK

These boxes beef up the sports knowledge that you've gained in the chapter. They give you an extra level of information and insight.

BET YOU DIDN'T KNOW

These are tidbits that are just fun to know, including the history of various sports or odd twists on rules.

Acknowledgments

Vicki Poretta wishes to acknowledge her husband, Joe, and their two children for their inspiration in the creation of the *Mom's Guide* series. Vicki also wishes to acknowledge John Rourke, Joe Fallon, and Henry Poydar of Big World Media, Inc., for their creative development and marketing of related *Mom's Guide* publications and products. She would also like to thank her friends at Poretta and Orr, Inc., especially Peter Laughton, for their creative help. Vicki also wishes to thank her many "sports mom" friends who lent their support and ideas along the cheering sidelines of their kid's games.

Deb Crisfield extends a big thanks to Gary Krebs at Macmillan for remembering her and knowing a good fit, and to Jennifer Perillo for seeing the book through production.

Deb also wants to thank the mothers and athletes who helped guide her through the few sports that have eluded her and her children so far: Meredith Ryder and her kids, Marshall, Courtney, James, and Christopher, who seem to have played more sports than any family on the planet; Nancy Wickenden, a great-grand-mother, grandmother, mother, and former headmistress of a prep school, who has sat through more sports than any person on the planet; Martha Wickenden, the former "Dear Abby" of tennis; Carrie Fettucine, soccer expert and Major League Soccer employee; Linda O'Malley, for her crew stories; Toby Proctor, a former wrestler who had some unprintable anecdotes; Walt Hulse, football contact; Carol Mullin, a volleyball player who came up with stories in other sports; Ranell Shea, the Hockey Mom; and Jennifer Benn, Lacrosse Mom and Mom to the incomparable Winston.

Deb also gives a huge thanks to her father for sticking that first racquet in her hand and to her mother for being the perfect role model for a Sports Mom and (almost) never missing a game.

And most of all, thanks to JAC, JDC, and CBC for hanging in there.

The View from the Bleachers

Some of the moms who have bought this book are looking for a quick review of the rules for a particular sport before the season starts. However, a whole host of others, just like you, need more than just the lowdown on one specific sport. This chapter is where you begin. It will help you choose a sport that fits the preferences and abilities of your child and your family. It also covers sports issues, such as cost and injury potential, that might not have occurred to you. Finally, it should give you a general idea of what programs are available for your child.

LET'S TALK SPORTS

Bats, pucks, sticks, cleats, shoes, kneepads, shinguards, mitts, rackets, clubs, helmets, and balls, balls, balls. Your house looks like the movie set from *Invasion of the Sports Equipment*. Your bank account is dwindling rapidly and you've spent so much time moving from the car to the field to the car to the court to the car to the rink that you're beginning to think you might have to get new address labels that read PVQ 684 Minivan Rd. You ask yourself: Is it all worth it?

The answer is a resounding YES! Kids and sports were meant for each other. Kids have boundless energy (except for that 5:00 hour right before dinner) and a natural, competitive desire to be the best at everything. Sports get them off the couch and often outside in the fresh air and give them many opportunities for friendship, teamwork, and leadership. Success in sports, either as individuals or as a team, can be a real ego boost for them (and failure teaches them valuable lessons, too).

Some parents worry about the competitive nature of many sports. Well, competition is a part of life. Your kids already deal with it every day with grades, friendships, and arguments over who has the better lunch or the cooler toy. Later in life, they're going to have to deal with college applications and the job market, two of the biggest competitions they'll ever face.

Organized sports can actually help kids learn how to deal with competition; they are supervised by adults who can show kids how to lose gracefully. (Of course, you hope that the adults can act like adults.) A good coach will ask athletes to try hard, do their best, and exhibit good sportsmanship.

WHAT HAVE I GOTTEN INTO?

Once you're comfortable with the whole idea of sports, you then have to figure out which sport (or sports) is best for you and your child. Here are some factors to consider before you make that decision:

◆ The interest factor

◆ The ability issue

◆ The travel time

◆ The injury potential

◆ The cost

Moms are going to have their own priorities when ranking these factors. It might be a good idea to figure out what yours are before you give your child freedom of choice.

The Interest Factor

First, and foremost, you should make sure it's your child who wants to play the sport and not you who wants her to play. A mother who once dreamed of being Chrissie Evert might assume that her daughter will feel the same way. However, buying her a tennis racket at age three, giving her lessons at six, and sending her to tennis camp at eight might frustrate the little girl, who instead dreams that she is Kerri Strug on the vault in the Olympics.

So ask your children what they want to play. They might surprise you. Children who are excited and interested in a sport are more likely to excel and have fun. If their answer is a shrug and an "I don't know," let them try one or two different sports each season. Some YMCA and YWCA classes (usually with names like "Sports and Games" or "Minor Leagues") cover several sports in one season.

Sometimes a parent just has to accept, however, that no sport will fit. Maybe young James Jr. inherited Great-Uncle Sidney's musical bent instead.

The Ability Issue

One father in my town was a strapping 6'4". He played college football and even had a tryout with a few pro teams. Football paraphernalia littered his house, and you always knew where to find him on Sunday afternoons. When he had his first son, nearly every baby gift was a football outfit. No one had any doubt that this baby was heading for the football field.

But it turned out that the little boy took after his mom, a petite 5'3" without much meat on her bones. Football practice in the Pop Warner league that his dad coached was torture for both the boy and his dad because the boy was crushed by the bigger athletes. Finally, the whole family agreed that soccer might be a better option.

This is a bitter pill to swallow. Your child might be desperate to play a sport for one reason or another, but you know it's a long shot. Give him a chance, but let him know there are other options. The skinny kid in football, the short kid in basketball, the heavy kid in soccer, and the ice hockey fan in Florida might be pretty miserable trying to find success in their chosen sport, but they might be happy elsewhere. Don't let a child give up on sports completely just because of a bad fit.

The Travel Time

When your child asks to play a sport, do some research to find out what sort of traveling demands it's going to put on you. Does your town have a recreation league volleyball program, or do you have to join a Y in the next town? Does the ice hockey team hold 6:00 a.m. practices in a rink that's 30 minutes away? Is your child's participation in the elite traveling soccer team worth spending your entire Saturday in the car, driving across the state to the opponent's town? Chances are your answer will be yes if your child is passionate about the sport. However, if you still haven't narrowed down the possibilities, you might want to consult other moms about car time before you commit.

The Injury Potential

Sports injuries are showing up everywhere and make many parents a little nervous. No one wants to see her child hurt, and the possibility of permanent damage is always there. But you need to take a look at *why* sports injuries are on the rise before you put the kibosh on all sports.

To begin with, kids are starting to play sports at a much younger age. It used to be that the only sports action young kids ever saw was in vacant lots, playgrounds, driveways, and backyards. Scrapes, bruises, stitches, or broken bones from this backyard play were labeled childhood injuries. Today, kids are getting into organized sports at younger and younger ages, and those same broken bones are now called sports injuries. The sport is blamed, rather than the rough-and-tumble, accident-prone nature of kids. In fact, organized sports are probably much safer than unsupervised play.

Overuse also contributes to the rise in injuries. Rather than becoming "three-sport athletes" and trying their hands (and feet) at different sports throughout the year, many young kids are specializing in one sport. They are repeating the same motion day after day throughout the year, which can be brutal on their bodies. Unless your child truly wants to focus on one sport, encourage a variety. By playing lots of sports, your child will exercise all his muscles, not just his pitching arm, for instance.

Finally, the rise in sports opportunities affects the rise in sports injuries. When I was in high school, there were few sports choices: football, basketball, and baseball for the boys and field hockey, basketball, and softball for the girls. In the spring, the track team was a fourth choice, but that was about it. These days schools offer soccer, volleyball, gymnastics, lacrosse, cross country, golf, wrestling, swimming, and ice hockey.

Girls are participating in sports in huge numbers now, and the growing number of rec league teams give kids of lesser ability a chance to continue to play after they've been cut from their high school team. All these changes mean a big increase in the number of young athletes, so it's hardly surprising that the number of sports injuries is rising, too.

TAKE A CLOSER LOOK

Here is a list of the injury potentials for the sports covered in this book:

Soccer: medium

Basketball: medium

Baseball: medium, but potential for overuse injury

Tennis: low, but potential for overuse injury

Golf: low

Lacrosse: medium for girls, high for boys

Ice hockey: high

Football: high

Volleyball: low

Wrestling: medium

The Cost

If your kids are playing school sports, the cost to you will be relatively small because the school usually picks up the majority of the tab. But if your kids are in town leagues or private sports, you could end up spending a bundle. It's just one more factor to consider when you and your children are making sports decisions.

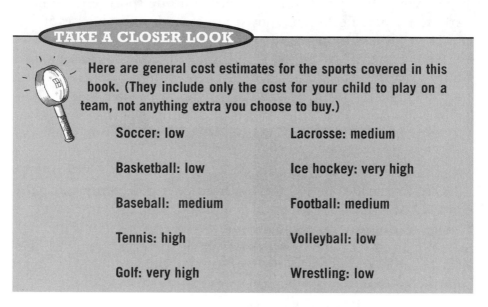

TAKE A CLOSER LOOK

Here are general cost estimates for the sports covered in this book. (They include only the cost for your child to play on a team, not anything extra you choose to buy.)

Soccer: low	Lacrosse: medium
Basketball: low	Ice hockey: very high
Baseball: medium	Football: medium
Tennis: high	Volleyball: low
Golf: very high	Wrestling: low

GET WITH THE PROGRAM

Once you decide on a sport, start checking out the local programs. Some towns have a few different options for kids to choose from. You should examine each to see which would be the best fit for your child. Here are some things to look for when you evaluate a sports program:

◆ Level of competition

◆ Coach's qualifications

◆ Time commitment

◆ Safety

◆ Money

Say you have a 12-year-old boy who wants to play basketball. The following sections describe how to find a good team for him.

School Program

At the most competitive level, there's probably a team at his junior high or middle school. He would have to try out for the team and probably be among the top 15 athletes to make it. If his junior high school has a *varsity* (top level) and *junior varsity* (second level) team (or even a *C team,* the third level), your child might have to be among only the top 30 or 50.

A school program would have a paid coach, who is trained in basketball, some first aid, and—if it's a public school—teaching. Because there is just one coach, you can ask around to get some feedback about him and his coaching style.

The time commitment for playing the sport would be every day after school, plus some evenings.

Safety would probably not be an issue because most schools now provide *trainers,* people who are familiar with sports injuries and first aid.

As for cost, the school would provide all the equipment, except for sneakers.

Recreation Department Leagues

If a school team isn't a good fit, then there might be a rec league program set up in your city or town. Call your town's Board of Recreation, Recreation Department, City Hall, or local schools to find out what programs area available. This kind of league usually has lots of teams, and anyone who signs up can play. If this choice is what interests you, call early. Some rec league signups begin months in advance of the season.

The coaches of rec leagues are usually parents of the children who are playing. They have little formal training, but if they volunteer to coach, chances are they're familiar with the game. Some towns do require their coaches to take a brief training class. If you know one of the parents who's coaching, the league might let you request him, but it's often hit or miss as to who you get.

The time commitment is much smaller, usually once or twice a week (one day for practice and one day for games is common), but it's usually on weekends or evenings, which might be precious time for your family.

The safety factor is a real issue. You might want to find out what first-aid training the coach has. It's unlikely that a trainer will be available, but the team should have access to a first aid kit, at least. Also, if you notice that the coach isn't having the kids stretch or warm up before they play, you might want to suggest that they do.

The cost will probably include a fee to sign up and, again, the sneakers; the rec league usually provides the equipment. Some coaches might think that the rec league doesn't supply enough equipment, so they could request that each player bring a ball to practice. If this isn't in your budget, you can talk to the coach about letting your child use one of the rec league balls.

Other Options

If your son has been cut from the school team and missed the signup for the rec league, or if he simply wants something instructional rather than competitive, there are still more options. Programs at the Y, rec centers, *intramurals* (organized after-school games that are open to all) at the school, and summer camps are all good choices.

The coaches in these programs are trained to some extent, at least in instruction techniques and first aid, if nothing else.

The time commitment varies. Classes at the Y might be held once or twice a week. The rec center and intramural programs might be a come-when-you-feel-like-it arrangement. Camps usually have intensive one-week or two-week programs.

Safety is generally not an issue. Most of these places have first-aid equipment and someone knowledgeable about safety and first aid somewhere on the premises.

Costs are generally high for the Y or for camps, but the programs would probably be free at your local school or rec center.

WHO'S AT THE HELM?

Finally, you've ironed out all the details. Your child has picked a sport, picked its venue, is on a team, and you're ready to go. Is there anything left to do?

Yes, absolutely! It's time for you to go be a fan. More than anything, children love having their parents as an audience. Read this book and learn all you can about the sport your child plays. Go to as many games as you can. You might even find yourself volunteering as a coach someday.

Besides the support you can give your child while you're in the bleachers, you have to be her advocate, too. Some coaches, even those with the best of intentions, can hurt kids physically and psychologically in their efforts to have a winning team.

When a child, especially one of the top performers on the team, gets hurt, some coaches might urge the child to "shake it off" or say "Don't be a wimp." Remarks like that aren't healthy for the child at all. If you're in the bleachers and notice that happening, ask that your child sit out for a while.

BET YOU DIDN'T KNOW

The five-minute rule is a good one to follow for all injuries, except for head and back injuries. Remove the child from the activity and have her rest for five minutes. If her injury is minor—she twisted her ankle or had the wind knocked out of her—five minutes is plenty of time for her to recover. If she can get up and play again, there's nothing to worry about. If she can't, it's doctor time. For head and back injuries, consult a doctor immediately.

Finally, make sure the coach is more of a cheerleader than a dictator. You want a coach who builds character, not conformity. The coach should also encourage good sportsmanship and fair play. Be on the lookout for a coach with a "win at all cost" mentality who suggests underhanded or overly aggressive tactics. You want your child to come away from the sport feeling great about it and herself.

That's not to say there shouldn't be some discipline or some eagerness to win on the field or court. Don't panic if your child's practices seem a little regimented. Basically, look for cues from your child. If your child is having fun, then the coach is doing the right thing, and the sport is a good experience for your child. The whole point of playing sports is to have fun.

THE LEAST YOU NEED TO KNOW

◆ Sports participation can build friendship, teamwork, and leadership.

◆ When you and your child choose a sport, consider interest, ability, travel time, injury potential, and cost.

◆ When you and your child choose a sports program, consider the level of competition, the coach's qualifications, the time commitment, the safety, and the cost.

◆ Make sure your child's coach emphasizes safety, good sportsmanship, and having fun.

Soccer: A Kick in the Grass

When your kindergartner announced that he wanted to play soccer, what was your reaction? Were you a true "soccer mom," embracing this up-and-coming sport, or were your memories of high school football games ringing the nostalgia bell, making you wonder if perhaps your son was choosing the wrong "football" game?

Well, if you were in the second camp, rest easy. Your son has it right. Soccer is on fire. I can't guarantee that it will catch up to football, but soon it will be as popular in the United States as it is in the rest of the world. Youth league soccer programs are everywhere, and the new Major League Soccer is providing soccer heroes galore for young spectators. Look out, football, soccer's on the move!

This chapter covers the ridiculously simple field and equipment and the fairly easy rules, from kickoff to a goal. It also delves into the much maligned and often misunderstood offsides rules. The different kicks are explained, the miles of restrictions for a throw-in are listed, and positions and formations are described.

TAKE A CLOSER LOOK

Look at some of the differences between football and soccer:

Football	Soccer
Elaborate rules	Simple rules
Expensive padding	Only shin guards
Strictly defined roles	Flexibility and opportunity
Lots of standing around	Constant exercise for the kid
Players develop thick necks and bodies	Players develop thin, muscled bodies
Injuries have caused paralysis and death	No paralysis, no death, an occasional black toenail

If your child is a girl, of course, it's a no-brainer—soccer is a better choice than football. Best of all, this sport is enormously fun.

PLAYING THE FIELD

If you want to learn the rules of soccer, begin by familiarizing yourself with the field, shown in the following diagram. The soccer field is rectangular (soccer fields vary in size) and divided in half by the *center line*. The purpose of the center line is to make sure each team is on its own side of the field at the start of each *kickoff*. After that, players have the whole field at their disposal, and the center line becomes irrelevant. Also used only at kickoff is the *center circle*, which bisects the center line and is used to keep the defending team (that is, the team not kicking off) ten yards away from the ball at kickoff.

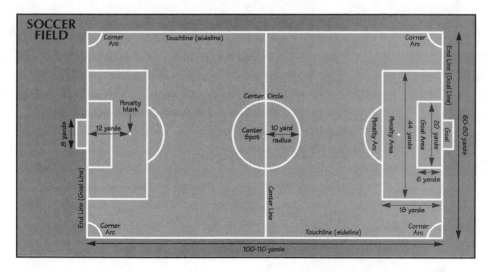

The soccer field.

The only other markings on the field are two boxes in front of each goal. The larger of the two boxes is 18 yards out from the endline (which you can see in the diagram) and is used to mark the goalkeeper's limits. Inside the box, the goalie is allowed to use his or her hands; outside the box, the goalie is just another field player (but don't ever tell a goalie that).

The other box is on the *six-yard line*. Within this box, the goalie can't be challenged when in possession of the ball. Primarily, though, this is where *goal kicks* (see "Getting Your Kicks" later in the chapter for an explanation) are taken. A hashmark between these two boxes, at the 12-yard line, is where *penalty kicks* (see the section "Getting Your Kicks" again) are taken.

That's the field. And if you think the field is simple, wait until I tell you about the equipment: Two goals and a ball—and that's it. Isn't that great? Although you should get your child a ball to practice with, you certainly aren't responsible for providing the goals (when necessary, trees or even sweatshirts work beautifully). Soccer is one of the cheap sports, so all moms on a budget should stick with it.

Some leagues require shin guards—which cost an extra five bucks—and your kids will probably lobby for cleats (a little more than five bucks), but in general the equipment list is limited to two goals and a ball.

PLAYING BY THE RULES

Even the rules (with the exception of "offsides") are simple. The object of soccer is to score more goals than the other team in 90 minutes of play. (The time is often shortened for younger players, but don't ask me why—they're the ones with all the energy.)

In her efforts to put the ball in the goal, any part of your child's body can be used to propel the ball, with the exception of the shoulders and everything protruding outward from them—in other words, arms and hands. A player who touches the ball with one of these outlawed parts will be called for a *handball*, which means the opponents get a free kick.

BET YOU DIDN'T KNOW

Occasionally, you might notice the refs ignoring a fairly obvious handball. Chances are they deemed it accidental, unavoidable, and not crucial to the outcome of the play. Under no circumstances should you let your children know that the refs sometimes do this because it will make them careless. Instead, tell your children to imagine their arms covered with sharp spikes, something to be kept away from an inflated ball at all costs.

The game is played with two teams of 11 players each: 10 field players and one goalkeeper. Goalkeepers are allowed to use their hands and must wear shirts of a different color from the rest of the team, so the refs can tell at a glance who is the privileged one. These days, goalkeepers have wild shirts. I'm not sure if all that diving on the ground has affected their fashion sense or if there's actually a strategy to it, like distracting the shooter with wild swirls of color. Either way, they certainly stand out in the crowd.

Play starts with the kickoff, won by the flip of a coin, with each team on its side of the field. As I mentioned before, the team not kicking off must stand outside the center circle. The ball must move forward once before anyone can move, and the player taking the first kick may not touch it again until someone else has touched it, which I hope explains that peculiar ritual you'll see your children performing at the start of the game. It always seemed crazy to me to see one player tapping the ball forward about a foot before another player took control and did something really productive. Once the ball is in play, the team passes, dribbles, and shoots the ball down the field.

When the players are high school, college, or professional, the progression down the field is a beautiful display of athleticism. When the kids are young, it's called chaos. Fortunately, there are some guidelines to protect budding Peles from maiming each other. The refs blow the whistle for pushing, kicking, tripping, striking, or holding another player. They also penalize players for making a dangerously high kick near someone's face or for lying down in the middle of the kicking frenzy. (Most players don't do this on purpose—they've usually fallen—but you never know.)

Finally, the refs monitor your children's behavior for poor sportsmanship and aggression. (Don't you wish you had a ref at home?) If your child does something unsportsmanlike, such as name calling, he gets a *yellow card*, which is a warning. If the child does it again, or if he commits a very aggressive foul, he gets a *red card*, which means he's no longer allowed to play in that particular game and the team may not replace him.

INSTANT REPLAY

I was at a soccer game not too long ago and heard a girl running down the field near the player who was dribbling, yelling, "I'm open! Pass me the ball." The other player, dribbling with her head down, complied. The only problem was that the girl who was yelling was on the other team. Immediately, the ref blew his whistle and gave the girl a yellow card for unsportsmanlike behavior. What a fabulously ethical sport!

Getting Your Kicks

When a player commits a foul, the other team is awarded a free kick. Teams also get free kicks when the ball goes over the endline (although not in the goal). The kicks have their own names, locations, and guidelines:

- ◆ **Direct kick**   This is a free kick awarded to a team when the other team commits a foul by pushing, kicking, tripping, charging, holding, or committing a handball. The direct kick is taken where the offense occurred.

- ◆ **Indirect kick**   This is a free kick awarded for less serious fouls, such as dangerous kicks, obstruction, poor conduct, and offsides (see "The Dreaded Offsides Rule" later in this chapter). The ball must be touched by two players before it can go in the goal; it's the only kick for which you specify how many players must touch the ball. Again, an indirect kick is taken where the offense occurred.

- ◆ **Penalty kick**   When the defense commits a "direct kick" foul within the 18-yard goal box, the offense chooses one person to take a kick from the 12-yard hashmark. All other players, except the goalie, must remain outside the box until the kick.

- ◆ **Drop kick**   When a referee needs to stop play for an injured player, a dog on the field, a bug in his eye, or any other odd event, play resumes with a drop kick. The ref drops the ball between two players of the coaches' choosing, and the ball must hit the ground before it's kicked.

- ◆ **Goal kick**   When the ball is kicked over the endline by the offense, defense gets a free kick, which is placed on the six yard line.

- ◆ **Corner kick**   When the ball is kicked over the endline by the defense, offense gets a free kick from the corner of the field on the side where the ball went out.

BET YOU DIDN'T KNOW

Nobody has been able to pinpoint the exact origins of soccer. Some people think cavemen played a form of it. The theory your kids will love the best, though, is that it started in England in the third century, when the Englishmen kicked the heads of conquered Danes through the streets.

BET YOU DIDN'T KNOW

Sometimes you'll see the kids line up shoulder to shoulder in front of a direct kick on the goal. This formation is called a *wall*. Although the players are required to be at least 10 yards away from the ball, the wall is a fairly effective method of blocking off the most accessible part of the goal. But take it from one who has been there: Standing in the wall is a slightly terrifying experience. Ten yards doesn't seem like much when you're facing a powerful kick. Take a look at the players in the wall. The boys have their hands down in front, and the girls have theirs across their chests. They know what to protect.

Throw-Ins

For some bizarre reason, the inventors of soccer—who remain unidentified just so they won't have to explain the throw-in—chose to use a *throw-in* to inbound a ball kicked over the sideline. In other words, the player picks up the ball with her forbidden hands and throws it back into play. This just doesn't make sense in a game where using your arms is taboo. The convoluted throwing method that all players must use further complicates matters:

◆ Both feet must remain on the ground for the duration of the throw.

◆ Both hands must be used equally.

◆ The ball must go fully over the thrower's head.

This awkward position must have been created to reinforce the point that arms are the awkward bad guys and should be avoided at all costs in favor of graceful, capable feet.

The Dreaded Offsides Rule

All the rules of soccer have been explained except the dreaded offsides rule. Every mom, new to soccer, has had the frustrating experience of seeing her child run down the field, way ahead of the defense, ready for a wide-open shot at a practically undefended goal, only to have her hopes dashed as the ref blows the whistle just as the child receives the ball. "Offsides," says the ref. And the other team gets the ball.

What exactly does *offsides* mean? The simple definition is that your child must have either the ball or two defensive players between him and the goal. This rule prevents a team from letting a player just hang around the goal until a teammate kicks the ball over the defense's head, something that's quite easy to do. That not only would be too easy a play, but it would also cut down on the intricate passing and creative moves a team must use to get the ball down the field. Without the offsides rule, soccer would look like a game of pinball.

Let's examine the two parts of the rule. If your child has the ball, he won't be offsides. Ever. So, if he dribbles by the last line of defense, then it's smooth sailing from there on in to the goal. Unfortunately, this doesn't happen too often, but it's perfectly legal.

The second requirement for preventing offsides is to have two defensive players between your child and the goal. One of the defensive players will, almost always, be the goalkeeper. Therefore, if your child doesn't have the ball, but is waiting to receive a pass, he must make sure there's a defensive player waiting there, too. The defensive player can be on the other sideline as long as he is closer to the goal than your child.

The rule gets a little more complicated when a pass is involved. If the player with the ball passes the ball forward, but not exactly to your child, your child can then zip by the defense in an effort to take possession of the ball. This move is allowed because the ball is still between your child and the goal, even though your child isn't exactly in possession of it yet.

Basically, the offsides rule keeps the players honest. Soccer players should play both offense *and* defense, and the offsides rule forces those goal-hungry forwards to drop back with their team-mates.

Who Does What Where?

When your daughter comes home from her first day of soccer prac-tice and tells you that the coach made her the *sweeper*, your first reaction might be panic. Is she cleaning up after the boys on her team? Very possibly. But is it with a broom? Not even remotely, so don't worry. The sweeper is just the last player in a long line of defense before the goalie. Her job is to "sweep" back and forth across the width of the field "cleaning up" the errors the people before her have made.

When the players line up on the field before the kickoff, you can tell from the bleachers that they've been arranged in some kind of formation. What that formation is depends on the strengths of the team and the preferences of the coach. The following sections describe some the more common formations.

The 4-3-3 Formation

The 4-3-3 formation is currently the most popular. The 4 refers to the defense. These defensive players are called *fullbacks*, and they set up in a diamond shape. The one nearest the goalie is the *sweeper*, who is placed in the center. The next two fullbacks are *wing fullbacks*; they are a little further up the field and near the sidelines. Slightly in front of them and centered on the field is the *stopper*.

The first 3 refers to the *halfbacks,* or *midfielders*, as they are often called. They are the link between the defense and offense and should play both offense and defense themselves. They are expected to cover the whole field. They set up as one center half and two wing halfbacks.

The last 3 refers to the forwards. They are up front, attacking the goal. They, like the halfbacks, have one center forward and two wings.

This formation works well when the skill level is pretty balanced on the team. All areas of the field are covered solidly.

A team with two exceptionally strong players might use the 4-2-4 formation. The two strong players would be the two halfbacks in the middle. This formation frees up another player for attack. The four forwards would probably set up in a diamond shape, similar to what the defense uses, with one very fast player waiting right at the edge of the defense, but not offsides, for a ball to be kicked over the defense's heads. This player is sometimes called a *striker*.

Actually, because of the way the players are lined up, the 4-2-4 formation looks more like 1-2-1-2-1-2-1, but that numbering scheme would be way too confusing for anyone to understand.

The 4-4-2 Formation

No coach likes to be forced into the 4-4-2 formation, but sometimes it's necessary with a weak team. In this case, the team is defense heavy, with only two forwards. This formation is also good for a team with a weak goalie, even if the rest of the team is fairly strong.

Chances are that a team playing a 4-4-2 formation won't get many goals, but the kids won't have to suffer the humiliation of a blow-out, either.

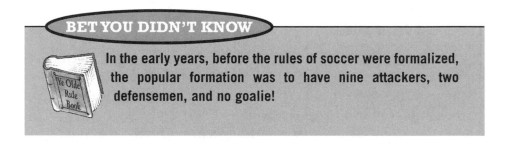

BET YOU DIDN'T KNOW

In the early years, before the rules of soccer were formalized, the popular formation was to have nine attackers, two defensemen, and no goalie!

BACKYARD FUN

Now you've turned yourself into a very knowledgeable soccer mom. You know the rules, you know the positions, and you've flipped ahead to the end of the chapter and have memorized all the cool soccer terms. You can sit in the bleachers and comment on how wonderful it was that Brittany's half-volley gave her a hat trick. But what happens when your child comes home, dying to play more soccer? You can't exactly invite the team over to your backyard.

Some great backyard games are explained in the following sections. The rules may differ wildly from the game you watch on the field, but the skills are the same, and any additional contact with the ball is going to be great for your child's development.

Pass for Points

Pass for Points is a great game for all age and skill levels. You'll need at least four players, but the more the better. Divide into two even teams. Pick a number from 2 to 8; the higher the skill level, the higher the number should be. Say you pick 4; the object of the game, then, is for one team to make four consecutive passes without the other team touching the ball—sort of an elaborate monkey in the middle. If the team succeeds, it gets one point. The first team to score 10 points wins.

Juggling

Juggling is more of a skill than a game, but it can easily be turned into a competition. The idea behind juggling is to keep the ball in the air using any legal parts of the body, such as the thigh, foot, or head. Have your child count how many touches he can make on the ball before it hits the ground. He should try to beat his high mark every time. If you're out there with him, he should try to beat your high mark (and vice versa). If he has a group of friends over, they can see who can touch the ball the most times.

If you have a group of people, have them stand in a fairly small circle and juggle the ball back and forth together. The starting player juggles the ball as long as she wants and then passes it to another player. There are two ways to turn juggling into a game. Again, the players can try to beat their high number, or they can turn it into an elimination game. The player in the group who lets the ball drop (the group can vote whether it's in a passing situation) steps out of the circle. The last player left at the end is the winner.

Ten and Again

Ten and Again is another fun skill builder; it's somewhat similar to dodgeball. You should have at least five players for it. One player starts in the center of a circle that's formed by the other players. They take a shot at him, and he tries to avoid it. If he can survive 10 kicks without being hit, he stays in the middle and gets to do it again.

Players on the outside are allowed to pass the ball to one another to set up a good shot, but they must first yell "pass" to distinguish the kick from one of the 10 shots that the middle player must survive. If a pass hits the middle player, it doesn't count.

The person who does hit the middle player on a shot gets to be the next person to go in the center, and the person who comes out of the middle starts the play.

LEARNING THE LINGO

It doesn't take long for moms to pick up on the new cool terms that kids are using in their everyday talk, but when a lot of new words are introduced with a sport, you might need some help. The following table lists some common soccer terms to complement your newfound offsides knowledge.

Common soccer terms	
TERM	*EXPLANATION*
advantage	When a referee allows a foul to occur without penalty, so the offensive team won't lose its advantage over the defensive team.
clear	When the defensive team kicks the ball far away from the defensive area, stopping the offensive drive to the goal.
cross	A pass from one side of the field to either in front of the goal or the other side of the field.
dribble	The way a player keeps the ball in her possession and moves it down the field. It's usually done on the ground with light taps from the player's feet.
forwards	Primarily offensive players. They begin the kickoff on the center line.
fullbacks	Primarily defensive players. They begin the kickoff nearest to the goalkeeper.
goalkeeper	The person who stands in the goal, wears a different-colored shirt, and is allowed to use his hands.
halfbacks	Also called midfielders. These players are the link between the fullbacks and the forwards. They are responsible for offense and defense and cover the whole field.

TERM	EXPLANATION
half-volley	Occurs when a player kicks the ball at exactly the same time it touches the ground.
hat trick	Three goals scored in one game by a single player.
heading	Hitting the ball with the forehead to make a pass or a shot on goal.
marking	Guarding an opponent.
nutmeg	Dribbling the ball between the defensive player's legs.
passing	Kicking the ball among players of the same team.
shooting	Kicking the ball with the intention of scoring.
slide tackle	Stealing the ball from an opponent by sliding into it on the ground. The sliding player must touch the ball first or it's considered a foul.
stopper	The frontmost defensive player.
sweeper	The last defensive player.
tackle	Stealing the ball away from another player.
throw-in	Inbounding the ball when it has been kicked over the sideline.
touch	Contact with the ball. In a two-touch pass, a player receives it with one motion and then uses a second motion to pass the ball to a teammate. A one-touch pass means the player received the ball and passed it all in one motion and with only one moment of contact with the ball.

continues

TERM	*EXPLANATION*
trapping	Taking control of the ball, especially when the ball is coming out of the air.
volley	Kicking the ball when it's in the air.
wall	A defensive structure, usually four players wide, in front of the goal. It's set up when the opponents are taking a direct kick and must be at least ten yards from the ball.
wings	The players positioned on the sides of the field. They can be forwards, halfbacks, or fullbacks.

Soccer is a game that spans all ages. The rules are simple, and beginners can have just as much fun as experts (if the two aren't playing together, of course). If you think you're going to have fun watching, you should try playing. Kids love an end-of-the-season Mom Challenge Match.

THE LEAST YOU NEED TO KNOW

◆ Soccer is a game between two teams of 11 players each.

◆ The object is to put the ball in the opponent's goal.

◆ The positions on the field are almost always divided into defensive players, offensive players, and midfielders, who connect offensive and defensive players. There's also a goalie.

◆ Soccer is accessible fun for everyone.

3

Slammin' Jammin' Basketball

In This Chapter

◆ The rules of the game

◆ Driveway fun

◆ Learning basketball lingo

Michael Jordan. Rebecca Lobo. Shaq Attack. March Madness. The Dream Team. Even the most sports-deficient mother has heard of one (if not all) of these. And even if the one you've heard of is Michael Jordan and he's familiar only because your eight-year-old dragged you to see *Space Jam* four times, the point still stands. Basketball has invaded our culture. Bye-bye, baseball...We've found a new national pastime.

The fast-moving pace of this fun new sport can, however, get in the way when a mom is trying hard to pick up the rules. This chapter puts the brakes on and takes you on a tour of the game at a much slower speed. You'll learn the rules, the fouls, the positions, and the plays, not to mention a few games for the driveway.

BET YOU DIDN'T KNOW

Basketball is one of the newest sports in history. Rather than evolving from caveman competitions or games in the Middle Ages the way other sports did, basketball was created in 1891 by James Naismith for a desperate YMCA. Workers at the Y needed an indoor winter sport to fill the time between football in the fall and baseball in the spring because calisthenics were all they had to offer, and the members were losing interest. (Can you blame them?)

ORDER IN THE COURT

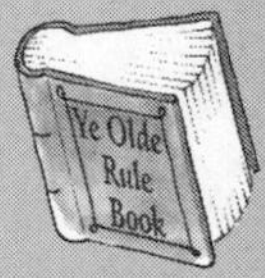

Generally speaking, the basketball you watch is played in the winter on an indoor court. That's not to say that basketball isn't played outdoors in the summer. (It better be, you say, after I shelled out $300 to install a hoop in our driveway.) But the outdoor courts at playgrounds, driveways, and city lots are more for pick-up games, which have their own rules. I'm going to delve into the real deal here.

Officially, a basketball court measures 84 feet long and 50 feet wide, although your child might be playing on something a little smaller, depending on the gym space available. There's one basket (actually, a metal hoop with a net hanging from it) at each end, suspended 10 feet above the court.

Fifteen feet into the court from the basket is a line called the *foul line* or *free-throw line*, where players get to shoot a free shot after being fouled. (See the following diagram.) This spot is also the scene of all basketball fantasies. You might see your child, alone in front of her driveway basket, muttering to herself, "There are two seconds left. We're down by one. I have to make one to tie, two to win the game…."

Arcing above the key, going from the base line back to the base line, is the three-point line. Any shot beyond this is worth three points instead of the regular two points.

The foul line also forms the top of a rectangle called the *key*. The court is divided in half by a center line, and in the middle of that is a circle used only at the start of a game (or the start of overtime) for the initial jump ball.

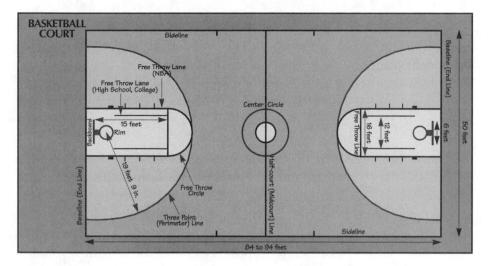

The basketball court.

BRING ON THE EQUIPMENT

If you're going to try playing basketball at home, you'll need at least one hoop and a basketball. Your child can wear pretty much anything, but most players wear shorts and a short-sleeve or sleeveless shirt. High-top sneakers are important because there's a lot of wear and tear on the ankles. Of course, be careful what you promise to buy or you could get caught in the sneaker wars, battling your child over his imagined need for $200 sneakers.

RULES TO LIVE BY

Basketball is played with two teams of five players each. In college, the game is played in two 15-minute halves. In high school, it's four eight-minute quarters, and in rec league ball, it's whatever the league decides.

The object of basketball is to score points by getting the ball through the hoop. Baskets are worth one, two, or three points. A shot from beyond the three-point line is worth three, a shot between the line and the basket is worth two, and a foul shot is worth one.

At the end of the game, the team with the most points is the winner.

Jump Right In

The game starts with a *jump ball*. The two tallest players (or the two who can jump the highest) take center court, and the rest of the team stands outside the circle. The referee tosses the ball high in the air, equally (she hopes) between the two center players, and they try to tap it to a teammate. They may not grab the ball themselves.

Jump balls used to be much more important in the game. In basketball's rookie year, the rules required jump balls after every basket, which slowed the game tremendously and gave a huge advantage to the taller team. The rule was quickly discarded, but there was also a rule requiring a jump ball after a disputed *possession* (in other words, the two opponents were still rolling on the floor, each with an arm around the ball). This rule was in effect until the mid-1980s. Now, (except in the pros) they just use a *possession arrow*, an electronic signal at the scorer's table, that points to one basket or another. When two players have the ball at once, the arrow dictates who gets the ball. Then it switches to the other direction for the next possession.

Most people are in favor of this change. It takes some of the advantage away from the tall teams, it doesn't rely on the (possibly poor) throwing ability of the referee, and it speeds up the game.

BET YOU DIDN'T KNOW

Most players of playground ball are happy to see the jump ball fall by the wayside. Aside from the difficulties of finding a competent, impartial tosser, the jumping players had to worry about the jump ball sneak attack: A group of 10-year-olds would grab onto a player's shorts seconds before he jumped up. Needless to say, when he went up, his shorts went down.

What the Hoop-la Is All About

Once the ball has been snagged by a team, the players head toward their basket with the intention of getting it in the hoop. There are three ways a player can move the ball closer to this goal:

◆ **Dribble**　Bouncing the ball on the floor, using only one hand at a time, while she moves up the court. A player may dribble for only one sequence during a possession. Once she picks up the ball, she's limited to the other two options.

◆ **Pass**　Throwing the ball to a teammate.

◆ **Shoot**　Tossing the ball in the direction of the hoop and hoping it swishes through the net.

A team has 10 seconds to move the ball up the floor, from its defensive end (the *backcourt*) to its offensive end. Once a player has brought the ball across the center line, the team may not take the ball back into the backcourt. Not that they really want to, but they've left that part of the court behind for good until it's time to play defense.

If a ball goes out of bounds, the team that did *not* touch it last gets to throw it back in bounds. This is called *inbounding*, and a player has five seconds to do it. A team also inbounds the ball after the other team has scored a basket. After a basket, the inbounding player may move anywhere along the baseline before throwing it in. If a player is inbounding after a ball went out of bounds, however, it has to be done from the spot where the ball went out.

Traveling Headaches

A basketball player may not, however, tuck the ball under his hand and race up the court like a football running back. Any time a player with the ball moves without dribbling, it's called *traveling*, and the other team gets possession.

Traveling reveals itself in other ways, as well. When a player is sprinting down the court on a *fast break*, he'll pick the ball up at the last second before he takes it up to the hoop. Given his momentum, he's bound to take a few steps on the way up. The refs will give him a little break, but taking two or three steps will bring on the traveling call.

Sometimes a player will dive on a ball on the floor. If she doesn't keep at least one of her feet anchored to the same spot, she's traveling. This call often seems especially unfair.

Finally, a player has to remember which foot is her *pivot foot*. If she's being guarded, she can move one foot as long as the other one stays put. The refs will call her for traveling if she pivots on the other one.

The Key to the Kingdom

The key, if you remember, is the area in front of the basket that extends out to the foul line. Obviously, it's the best place to be, whether you're shooting, rebounding, or defending. The rules of basketball have conspired, though, to make it a little less desirable for the shooters.

An offensive player, shooting or not, may be in the key for only three seconds at a time. However, he can be in for three seconds, step out for half a second, and then go in for three more. The rule just keeps players moving.

You'll notice that this rule affects only certain kids. There are two types of young basketball players: the ones who run around like chickens with their heads cut off and the baskethangers who just wait by the hoop for a chance to shoot. The chickens might not spend even one second in the key, but the baskethangers have a tough time remembering to move away. If your child is a baskethanger, you'll become very familiar with this rule.

INSTANT REPLAY

A young player I know named Perry was always getting called for the three-second rule. It drove his father crazy until he finally came up with a plan. He brought Perry's younger brother to the game and pulled out ten singles in front of the two boys. "Perry," he said, "this money is yours at the start of the game. But every time you get called for three seconds, one of these bills goes to your brother." Perry was never called for three seconds again.

Foul Play

The defensive team does its best to stop the ball from going in their opponent's hoop. The players wave their arms, steal passes, slap the ball away from sloppy dribblers, and block shots. They can do nearly anything as long as they don't touch their opponents, or so the rules say.

In reality, the refs allow for quite a bit of body contact, especially between two players who don't have the ball. You'll see them leaning into each other, maybe throwing elbows to get into a better position, pushing off, and more. You'll probably want to run onto the court to help your kid because the refs certainly don't seem to care, but really, a little of this contact is acceptable.

If the player has the ball, though, it's a completely different story. Just about any contact—a slap as a player is trying to steal the ball, a swat at the ball that ends up on the shooter's arm, a body check as the defender tries to keep the player from driving to the hoop—will prompt the referee's whistle.

When a foul is called, play stops and the clock stops. If the foul was committed against a shooting player, then that player gets to go to the foul line for some free shots. For an interrupted two-point shot, she gets two free shots; for a three-point shot, three shots. If the player was fouled and her shot still went in, she gets to take only one foul shot. Each foul shot is worth one point.

Sometimes, obviously, the foul is committed somewhere else on the court. In that case, it's a little more complicated:

◆ First, the number of team fouls is checked.

◆ If a team has less than five fouls, the ball is taken out of bounds for a restart.

◆ After the fifth foul, the player is given a *one-and-one shot*. When a player takes a one-and-one shot, he shoots one foul shot. If he makes it, he gets another; if he misses, normal play resumes with the rebound.

◆ After the fifth foul, with only two minutes left in the game, the player is given two shots.

Foul shots can be real gifts. A team that practices foul shooting will be a team that wins.

PLACES EVERYONE

Each team has five players. Unlike soccer, hockey, football, and many other sports, the five players are entirely on defense or entirely on offense. No one hangs back to protect the goal or stays forward, waiting for a chance to score. That said, I'm sure you'll notice plenty of kids who think their only job is to score. The glamour in defense is sometimes hard to find.

Although all five players are involved in both offense and defense, each one does have his own role. On each team, there's usually a *center*, one or two *forwards*, one or two *guards*, and a *point guard*. Sometimes a player is a guard on offense and a forward on defense, or vice versa, but the responsibilities are the same.

The Center of Attention

The center is the big kid. Because of her height, she can get the closest to the basket. A team usually tries to position her near the basket on both offense and defense. On offense, she has to remember the three-second rule and move in and out of the key, but on defense, she just hangs underneath and looks for a rebound. Shaquille O'Neal, Patrick Ewing, and Rebecca Lobo are centers.

Moving Forward

The forwards are next in line as far as height is concerned. They also play down low near the basket. If a team is using one forward, then he takes up the position on the opposite side from the center. If the team is using two forwards, then they'll usually flank the center on either side of the key. Larry Bird, Sheryl Swoopes, and Carl Malone are forwards.

I Get the Point

The point guard is the general of the army, the CEO of the company, the mom of the house—in other words, the person who runs the show. She brings the ball up the court, runs the plays, and is often a good outside shooter. The point guard is the team's best ball handler. She can dribble well, pass well, and keep her head up during all the action, making sure the right play is being run. Jason Kidd and Nancy Lieberman are point guards.

On Guard

The guards are the shortest players on the team. Ideally, they are very quick and are good passers and shooters. Most of the time, they are positioned at the top of the key. On defense, they are the front line, and they try to stop a play before the ball gets anywhere near the basket. Penny Hardaway, Magic Johnson, and Michael Jordan are guards.

ZONING OUT AND OTHER DEFENSIVE TRICKS

In general, there are two defensive strategies that teams take: either a *man-to-man* (or in these more politically correct times, a *person-to-person*) *defense* or a *zone defense*.

Think of two families, each consisting of a mother and father, but one family has two children and the other has three. In the two-child family, the parents can take a man-to-man approach: "Okay, you have James for the morning, and I'll take Corinne." In other words, one parent per child.

When you move over to the three-child family, the defense shifts to a zone. "You stay home with a napping Ryan while I drive Katie and Pete to piano lessons. Then I'll take Ryan and Pete to the park, while Katie has her playdate at home with you." This strategy is a zone defense. One parent covers the home zone, and the other parent covers the carpool zone.

In basketball defense, it's the same. Each player is responsible for either an opposing player (if it's man-to-man defense) or an area on the court (if it's zone defense).

Occasionally, a team tries a combination of man-to-man and zone defense if there's an excellent player on the other team. One variation is called a *box-and-one*, in which four players form a zone defense box around the key and the one leftover defender plays man-to-man with the superstar on the other team.

INSTANT REPLAY

During the final game of the NBA championships between the Boston Celtics and the Milwaukee Bucks, the Celtics came up with a new kind of defense. Kareem Abdul Jabbar had been killing the Celtics in earlier games. The rest of the team had barely contributed anything. It was time to gang up, so they created what's now known as "The Sag." All the Celtic players dropped back off their men (they were playing man-to-man defense) and created a ring of defenders around Jabbar. The other men were left open, but they couldn't hit the shots. They were all used to Jabbar scoring the points.

PLAY BY PLAY

Offense is a little more complicated than defense. Once a team sees what defense its opponents are using, it decides what plays to use to attack them. The point guard (or sometimes the coach) calls the play. These plays are designed to move the players and the ball in a certain pattern around the floor. With luck, the defense gets thrown off-guard, and an open shot or a lane to the basket is freed up.

Against a person-to-person defense, a team might try to block one player's defender, freeing that player up for a pass, a jump shot, or a drive to the hoop. This blocking is called a *pick*. Another related term is the *pick and roll*, which means that the person who just picked off the defender "rolls" or turns toward the basket as a second option for that pass. Basically, the point of this type of move is to get in the way and confuse the defenders who are trying to stay with their players.

Another popular move against a person-to-person defense is a shift of all the players to one area, freeing up a whole side of the court. One person cutting in the other direction then has an open shot.

When it's a zone defense, it's a different story. The pick and roll and the shifts aren't going to work because the defenders don't move much with the players. Against the zone, quick passes and constant shifts in position are the tactics. The idea is to move players and the ball around so fast that the defense, not knowing what the play is, gets caught out of position trying to keep up.

Coaches and players should learn the offensive plays for attacking both kinds of defense. You never know what the other team is going to throw at you. They might even use a *full-court press*, which means they start putting pressure on the ball before it's even inbounded!

The following sections describe some great games the kids can play with you or with their friends.

Horse

Horse is a great game for kids of all ages because it can be taken seriously or turned into silly fun. It works best with two to four players. The first player takes a shot from anywhere on the court. If he misses, then the next player can take any shot he pleases. However, if the first player makes the shot, then the next player must duplicate that shot exactly.

If the second player makes this same shot, then the first player (or subsequent players) must make the shot again. This sequence goes on until someone misses, and that person gets an *H*. The next person in line decides which shot will be tried next. Play continues in this manner until someone has spelled out *H-O-R-S-E* and is the loser. The other players continue until only one is left.

Shots don't have to be the conventional "jump shot from the corner." I've always done my best scoring by using a left-handed hookshot with my eyes closed.

Twenty-one

Twenty-one can be played by all ages and all skill levels. It can also be played with an unlimited number of people. To set the game up, grab some sidewalk chalk and draw an arc on the driveway around the hoop. The distance out from the basket depends on the skill of the players.

The first player takes a shot from behind the chalk line. If she makes it, she gets three points. However, whether or not she makes it, she rushes in to get the ball, no matter where it is, and shoots again. This shot is worth two points. The final shot is a lay-up worth one point. Then it's the next player's turn.

Each player, therefore, can earn 0–6 points in each turn. Play continues until one player reaches 21 points. The hitch is that a player must hit 21 on the nose, so she might have to miss a few on purpose.

LEARNING THE LINGO

Someone could probably fill an entire book with the basketball slang that's used now, so don't expect that here. The following table covers just the basic terms you might need when you're trying to tell your son that you liked the way he was tough on defense.

Basketball lingo	
TERM	*EXPLANATION*
backboard	The board behind the basket.
backcourt	The defensive side of a court. Obviously, it's different for each team.
boxing out	Putting your body in a position that keeps the other team from getting the rebound.
center	Usually the tallest player on the team. Stands near the basket on both offense and defense.
double dribble	Dribbling, stopping, and then trying to dribble again in the same possession.
dribbling	Bouncing the ball one-handed.
fast break	Racing down the floor and taking the ball to the hoop ahead of the defense.
forward	The position for the taller players on the team, usually on the sides of the basket.
foul line	The line at the top of the key where the foul shots are taken.
foul shot	A free shot given to a player after a foul.
free throw	Another term for foul shot.

TERM	EXPLANATION
guard	The position for the smaller, quicker players.
inbounding	A pass that puts the ball back onto the court after the ball has gone out of bounds or after a shot has been made.
jump ball	The way the game begins. The ball is tossed in the air between two players who try to tap it to teammates.
key	A six-foot wide area between the foul line and the base line.
lay-up	A close shot, usually done on the run.
one-and-one	A foul shot where the player gets a second free throw if the first one goes in.
passing	Throwing the ball to another teammate.
pivot foot	The foot that remains in one spot while the rest of the body moves. A player needs a pivot foot only when he has the ball and isn't dribbling it.
point guard	The ball handler of the team.
possession arrow	The arrow that shows which team gets the ball when two players are both holding on to it.
rebounding	Retrieving the ball after a missed shot.
shooting	Throwing the ball toward or into the basket.
traveling	Moving both feet while in possession of the ball without dribbling the ball.

James Naismith knew he was doing the Y a favor when he filled their request for a winter sport with the game of basketball, but he probably never envisioned what a gift the game would be to the world of sports and especially to moms. It's not too violent, it's not too complicated, it's not too expensive, and it's played in a climate-controlled environment. Hard to beat!

THE LEAST YOU NEED TO KNOW

◆ Basketball is played with two teams of five players each.

◆ The object of the game is to score more baskets than the other team.

◆ All five players on a team play as an offensive unit when they have the ball and as a defensive unit when the other team has it.

◆ The sport's fast pace and relatively low injury rate makes it fun for kids and moms alike.

The Pitch for Baseball

Baseball, once the national pastime, has recently fallen out of favor. The strikes, the players' high salaries and arrogant attitudes, and the high prices at the ballfields have turned kids away from the pros. Without a Babe Ruth, Mickey Mantle, or Hank Aaron to inspire them, kids have less drive to pursue baseball themselves. Cal Ripken is probably the best-known baseball hero in today's game, and his achievement of the most consecutive games played, although impressive, hardly gets kids' juice pumping.

Baseball also has to compete with a growing plethora of spring sports. Lacrosse is starting to catch on. Track is big, and tennis is gaining in popularity. Out of school, there's also golf and soccer to claim a kid's time.

So where does all this leave baseball? I think it still has a chance. Minor league teams are gaining in popularity, and if the pros can get their act together, they might recapture some lost fans. Baseball has a history that can't be easily forgotten—and shouldn't be.

This chapter will take you from start to finish, dugout to outfield. You'll learn the nuances of the baseball diamond and the names of the positions. The rules, like the infield fly rule, are explained, as are baseball's other little quirks. You'll also learn about Little League elbow, a very preventable but dangerous injury. A quick look at softball, the stats obsession, and the lingo wrap it up.

BET YOU DIDN'T KNOW

 Credit for inventing baseball has often been given to Abner Doubleday of Cooperstown, New York (site of the Baseball Hall of Fame), but that's just a story made up to give baseball some history at a time when it didn't have much. However, now we can admit that we know little of its origins: Baseball evolved from cricket, the first recorded game was played in Hoboken, New Jersey, and a man named Alexander Cartwright was the first to write the rules down officially.

A DIAMOND IN THE ROUGH

Baseball is played on a two-part field: the *infield* (called the *diamond*) and the *outfield*. (See the following diagram.) The infield consists of a pentagonal *home plate* (or *home*) and three square *bases*; these four points are each 90 feet apart and form a square. Going in a counterclockwise direction, the bases are referred to as *first base*, *second base*, and *third base*. In the center of this square (or diamond), 60 feet and 6 inches from home plate, is the *pitcher's mound*.

The diamond is either all dirt or dirt on the base paths and grass in the center. The outfield is a grassy area extending outward beyond the infield. Many fields have walls or fences to mark the end of the outfield, but others let the outfield continue indefinitely.

Two white lines define the side boundaries of the field. They are called the *foul lines*, and they lead away from home plate into the outfield. The line on the left of home plate touches the outside of third base, and the line on the right touches the outside of first base.

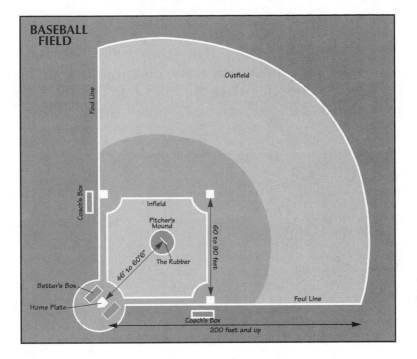

BASEBALL FIELD

Outfield

Foul Line

Coach's Box

Infield

Pitcher's Mound

60 to 90 feet

46' to 60'6"

The Rubber

Batter's Box

Home Plate

Foul Line

Coach's Box

200 feet and up

The baseball field.

LOAD ON THE EQUIPMENT

Baseball requires lots of equipment, but fortunately, most of it will be supplied by the leagues your child plays on. You will have to supply the *glove*, or *mitt*, a leather, hand-shaped device that helps a player catch the ball without pain. You might have to buy *cleats*, too.

The other equipment that's needed is a bat, a ball, and helmets for the batters and baserunners. Usually, the team supplies several bats because they come in different weights and lengths for players of differing strengths and abilities. One player, called a *catcher*, needs a face mask, a chest protector, and shinguards. The organization will supply these, too, and might even supply the special catcher's glove, which has more padding.

PLAYING THE FIELD

There are nine players on each team. (See the following diagram.) At the start of the game, the *home team* positions itself in the field and is considered the defensive team. It's up to the home team to prevent the other team from scoring.

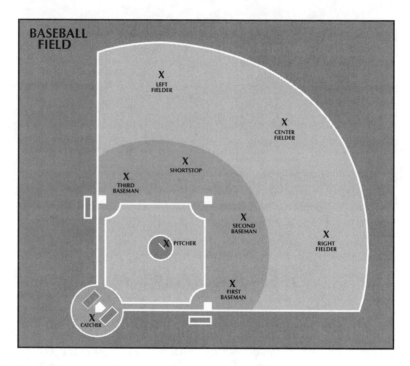

Baseball positions.

The infield has six positions: one player guarding each of the three bases (called the *first baseman, second baseman,* and *third baseman*), a player between second and third (called the *shortstop*), a *pitcher*, and a *catcher*.

The pitcher has initial control of the ball. It's his job to throw the ball over home plate. The catcher is positioned behind home plate, and his main job is to catch the pitcher's ball if the batter doesn't hit it.

The outfield has three positions: *left fielder, center fielder,* and *right fielder.*

The other team, the *visiting team,* gets the first chance at batting. The players sit in their *dugout* (usually just a bench in the younger leagues), waiting for their turn to bat. They go up one at a time to try to hit the ball thrown by the pitcher. The players must bat in the order they're listed or it's an automatic out.

INSTANT REPLAY

During one Little League game, a mom was in charge of the batting order for her son's team. In typical mom fashion, she was also chief nurse and chief cheerleader for the team and was busy doing both for a sad, injured boy in the ninth inning when she sent the wrong boy up to bat with two outs and the bases loaded. Well, the mistake was immediately caught by the opponents. The team was given an automatic out and the game was over. Life is unfair sometimes, isn't it?

PLAY BALL!

Given that no one is quite sure of baseball's origins, I'm convinced that a brother and sister team, somewhere around the age of eight, came up with the rules. They are so convoluted that they sound like two siblings making up a game. It's almost impossible to decide where to begin, but if I must, I must.

Take Me Out to the Ball Game

Play begins with a *pitch* from the pitcher, who throws the ball in the general direction of the batter and home plate. The batter, if he likes the pitch, swings and tries to hit the ball into the field. Once he has hit the ball, he tries to run around the bases. To score, a player must start at home plate, touch every base, and come back to home plate, touching it, too. That trip around the bases counts as one *run*. It can be done all at once or in several turns, base by base.

While the batter is trying to score, the defensive team is trying to get him *out* in one of these four ways:

- If the batter hit the ball in the air, the defensive players can catch it before it hits the ground.

- If the ball has already touched the ground, they can get the ball to the base before the batter gets there. (The ball doesn't have to touch the base itself. It's good enough if the player holding the ball is touching the base.)

- They can *tag* the runner with the ball. Any runner who is not on base can be tagged. Runners are safe only when they're on a base.

- The pitcher can strike the batter out. A *strike* is a pitch that goes over home plate at a level between the batter's knees and shoulders. Whether the batter watched it go by or swung for it and missed, it counts as a strike. An impartial *umpire* stands behind the plate to judge the pitch. A player is allowed three strikes before he's called out.

The defensive team need three of these outs to get its turn up to bat. Ideally, it would like to get these outs before the other team gets runs.

Up to Bat

A batter has three options for getting to base:

- He can hit a ball that drops onto the field far from the fielders, so they can't retrieve the ball and get it to the base before him. The batter runs fast to get to as many bases as possible before the fielders retrieve the ball. He stops when he thinks they might be able to get him out at the next base. The umpire determines whether the batter beat the ball to the base. A tie is always given to the runner.

- He can get hit by the pitch, but don't suggest this method to your children. It's such an unfortunate and painful occurrence that the batter gets to go to first base for free.

- He can *walk*. It's called a walk when the pitcher throws four pitches to the batter that aren't strikes. They are called *balls*.

A batter has to watch a pitch go by for it to count as a ball. If he swings at it and misses, it counts as a strike, even if it was a terrible pitch. When a player walks, he can go to first base only, and then he has to wait for the next player to move him along.

INSTANT REPLAY

One very little Little Leaguer couldn't hit the ball if his life depended on it. In fact, he could barely hold up the bat, much less swing it. He hadn't gotten on base once in the first four games of the season. Then, his first time up to bat in the fifth game, thud! He was hit by a pitch and got to go to first base. It changed his baseball career. After that, every time he was up to bat, he stood so far back and crouched down so low that the pitchers had a hard time throwing strikes. He got on base nearly every time with a walk and became a valuable member of the team.

A ball doesn't count as a hit unless it's hit between the two foul lines. If the ball is hit outside the foul line, it's called a *foul ball*. A ball can also roll foul, if it rolls over the foul line before it gets to first or third base. If it rolls over the line in the outfield, it's considered a *fair ball* and therefore playable.

A foul ball counts as a strike, although it can never be the third strike. A player can foul an unlimited number of balls and still be at strike two. The only time a foul counts as the third strike is when a player *bunts* it foul. (Don't worry, bunts are explained later.)

Covering the Bases

After the first batter is either out, on base, or back in the dugout after scoring a run, the next batter goes up to bat. He tries to get on base, too, and if there's someone already on base, he hopes to hit the ball so that person can get all the way home. Only one person per base is allowed. This rotation continues until the fielders manage to get three outs. After three outs, the teams switch places.

After both teams have been up to bat and gotten three outs each, an *inning* has elapsed. A game consists of nine innings. If the score is tied at nine innings, then the game goes into more innings until one team scores more runs than the other. Both teams must have had their chance to bat in the inning, however; it's not a sudden-death kind of thing.

Running Wild

The act of baserunning is slightly more complicated than my overview of the rules implies. When a player is on base, he must run to the next base if someone is heading to his base. If no one is forcing him, he can stay at the base he's on if he thinks he's going to get out.

Say there's a runner on second base and no one on first. The batter hits the ball to the shortstop, who is right in the baserunner's path to third. Chances are he's going to want to stay at second, at least until the shortstop throws the ball to first base. Now picture that same guy at second base, but there's also someone on first. When the ball is hit, both runners must run. The batter is heading to first, pushing that guy off first and onto second, who is pushing the guy on second forward to third base.

If a player is forced to run, then the defensive player merely tagging the base the player is going to counts as an out. The player himself doesn't have to be tagged, but if he is, it's still an out. If the player isn't forced to run, however, then the player needs to be tagged, instead of the base.

If the ball is caught in the air (which is an out), a player who has left a base must go back to the original base and touch it after the ball is caught. If he's halfway to the next base, thinking the ball won't be caught, he must turn around and go back. If the other team can get the ball to the base before the baserunner gets back, then it's another out. That's one way to get a *double play*. A double play is two outs for one turn at bat.

If the ball has been hit way out to the outfield, however, a player might choose to *tag up*, meaning he waits on the base until the ball has been caught. The second it's in the defensive player's glove, he then takes off for the next base. You see, he was touching the base after the fly ball was caught, but then he hopes to beat out the throw to the next base. Given that it's not a force play, he, not the base, must be tagged, which makes it even harder for the other team to get him out. Tagging up is very common.

Stealing the Show

Base stealing is similar to tagging up; essentially, it means running for a base at some time other than on a hit. Most stolen bases happen while the pitcher is in his windup. If the runner is fast enough, he can get to the next base before the ball gets from the pitcher to the catcher to the baseplayer. Second base is the most common one to steal because it's the farthest throw for the catcher. Stealing home isn't really a good bet, for obvious reasons.

Players can move off the base to help them on their way to a steal; this is called *taking a lead*. They need to touch the base again after every pitch, but can then inch away as far as they feel comfortable. They don't want to go too far, or the pitcher will throw to the base rather than the plate and they'll be out. Most players go a couple of yards out.

Deciphering the Infield Fly Rule

There's one more rather complicated rule that was added to solve a little glitch in the game. The rule is called the *infield fly rule*, and although its definition sounds ridiculous, it's one of the more important changes to the game. It says if a ball is hit in the air in the infield with less than two outs and there are runners on base, then it's an automatic out for the batter whether or not the ball is caught. Right now, you're probably sitting there slack-jawed, wondering what on earth that meant, so I'll give you an example.

Picture this. Your child is the runner on first base. His teammate hits a little pop fly to the infield. It's an easy catch, so your child just takes a small lead off the base because he figures he's going to have to touch first base again once the ball is caught. All of a sudden, the fielder misses the catch. Now your son is forced to run to second because the batter is heading for first. The fielder scoops up the dropped ball, fires it to the second baseman, who then fires it to the first baseman. Now, instead of the one out for the pop fly, the team has gotten two outs, one for the force play at second and one for the force play at first.

You might say, why couldn't my son anticipate this and sprint to second before the ball is missed? The answer is easy. The fielder would then have just caught the ball and thrown it to first, again for a double play. To solve this, the infield fly rule states that if this happens, the batter is called out.

It's an infield-only rule because when the ball is hit in the outfield, the runner has more time either to go back or to go on. In fact, when a fly ball goes to the outfield, most players run halfway between the two bases to wait and see which way to run next.

The rule is in effect only when a team has less than two outs because there's no need for a double play with two outs, so none of this would happen. The runner would be running all out no matter what. And if there's no runner on base, then there's no force play and again, it's not an issue. So, as convoluted as it is, the rule does make sense.

BET YOU DIDN'T KNOW

In the early days of the game, the *substitution rule* read, "A player may be substituted into the game at any time as long as the umpire is notified first." One player named Mike Kelly stretched the limits of this rule. A ball was popped up near the dugout. It didn't look as if the regular catcher was going to catch the ball before it hit the ground. Mike Kelly yelled, "Kelly in at catcher!" and ran out and caught the ball. The rule was immediately changed to read, "Substitutions are only allowed when the ball is not in play."

HERE'S THE PITCH

There are lots of fancy pitches, but for inexperienced players, just getting the pitch over the plate is an accomplishment. As your young pitcher gets more skilled, here are some of the pitches you might hear him talk about:

◆ **Fastball**   A straight pitch with lots of velocity.

◆ **Knuckleball**   A ball with no spin.

◆ **Changeup**   A pitch whose delivery looks like a fastball but that actually comes in much slower.

◆ **Breaking ball**   A catchall term for a ball that curves in some way. The next three pitches are types of breaking balls:

- ◆ **Curveball** A ball whose trajectory loops both downward and outward.

- ◆ **Slider** A ball that curves in or out at the last minute.

- ◆ **Sinker** A ball that drops down at the last minute.

The better pitchers can vary the pitch's speed and throw the ball low or high or inside the plate (closer to the batter) or outside the plate (far away from the batter). At the highest level of baseball, pitchers know what type of ball the batter can hit and what type the batter has trouble with. That's how pitchers decide what pitch to throw. At the middle level, however, they just vary their pitches, hoping to catch the batter off guard.

When a pitcher is on the mound with the ball, he might choose to throw to a base, hoping to catch a runner who has taken too big a lead. The pitcher can do this only before he has begun his pitching motion, however. If he ever stops his pitching motion for any reason, it's called a *balk* and the batter is given an automatic ball.

Batter Up

Batters also have several options:

- ◆ **Single** A hit that gets them to first base.

- ◆ **Double** A hit that gets them to second base.

- ◆ **Triple** A hit that gets them to third base.

- ◆ **Home run** A hit that gets them all the way around the bases for a run. A home run could also (more likely) be a hit that goes over the fence or wall, which is an automatic home run.

- ◆ **Bunt** A hit in which the batter doesn't swing at the ball; instead, he just pushes the bat at the ball. The intention is to get the ball to drop on the ground near the foul line halfway between the catcher and the first or third baseman.

- ◆ **Sacrifice fly** A long fly ball to the outfield that allows a base runner on third to tag up and go home to score. In other words, the player sacrifices his turn at bat to get his team a run.

TAKING A CLOSER LOOK

Because the home run is the glory hit in baseball, it has a ton of other names. If your child starts talking about homers, roundtrippers, dingers, taters, four-baggers, or grand salamis, you'll know she means home runs.

The first four hits in the list are luck of the draw. The batter can never be sure how far he's going to get until he's actually running the bases. The other two hits, however, are conscious decisions. If a coach wants a player to choose one of these hits, he usually signals the player to do so.

THE ENDLESS STATS

There are a ton of baseball statistics, and your child will be spouting hers off to you throughout the season. You'd better know about a few of the biggies—*batting average*, *RBIs*, *ERA* (no, it's not the Equal Rights Amendment)—before you congratulate her on her .200 batting average.

◆ **At Bats (AB)**   The number of times your child came to the plate, although sacrifices and walks don't count as at bats.

◆ **Hits (H)**   The number of times your child connected with the ball in a way that she was able to get on base. A fly ball caught by the center fielder might look pretty, but it doesn't count. A *worm-burner* that just skids along the infield ground but eludes the fielders does count. If your child got on base because of a fielder's error, however, it doesn't count in the hit total.

◆ **Batting Average (BA)**   The number of hits divided by the number of at bats, taken to the third decimal point. For instance, if your child had four at bats in a game and got a hit two of those times, her batting average would be .500, which is very good. Anything over .300 is very good. The expression "batting a thousand" comes from the terminology for batting average statistics and means no misses. (Just so you know, nobody bats 1.000.)

◆ **Runs Batted In (RBI)**   A tally of the players who scored during your child's at bats. For instance, if there were two people on base and your child hit a double, bringing both of them home, then she gets two RBIs. If she hit a home run, she gets three because she brought herself home, too.

◆ **Earned Run Average (ERA)**   A pitcher's stat. An *earned run* is a run specifically given up by a pitcher rather than a run a team got because of an error made by a fielder. (In Little League, it's not unusual to have even a bunt turn into a home run because of all the throwing and catching errors.) An ERA under four is considered good.

There are also stats for hits, walks, doubles, triples, home runs, home run average, slugging percentage, on base average, hit by pitches, fielding average, wild pitches, strikeouts, hits while runners are on base, hits into double plays, strikeouts with runners on base, and on and on.

REC LEAGUE BALL

When your child starts baseball, chances are he'll be playing tee-ball first. In tee-ball, pitching is eliminated. The ball is set up on a prop, called a *tee*, and the batter hits it off. This prop helps for two reasons. It's easier for beginning players to get a hit, and you don't have to worry about endless walks from an inexperienced pitcher.

The next step after tee-ball is normal baseball, but with the coach of the batting team acting as the pitcher. A "pitcher" from the other team stands on the mound to be the fielder if the ball is hit that way. After this kind of baseball, kids then graduate to Little League, Pony League, and American Legion ball.

LITTLE LEAGUE ELBOW

One of the downsides of being a baseball mom is that you have to be very aware of how much your young pitcher is throwing. Pitchers can't pitch every day because they will ruin their arms. In fact, *Little League elbow* is actually a medical term because it has become so common.

In adults, tendons attach muscles to bones, but in kids, these tendons are usually attached to the growth cartilage that has yet to turn into bone. Because the cartilage is soft, constant snapping of the tendons (a motion that happens when a pitcher pitches) might tear some of this cartilage. This tearing causes some pain that will only get worse if the arm isn't rested immediately. If your little pitcher is saying his elbow hurts, take him to a doctor right away.

To prevent this injury, Little Leaguers are allowed to pitch only six innings a week. This rule is smart from a medical standpoint, and it also gives lots of kids the opportunity to pitch. Most coaches adhere to the rule, but often the overuse problem comes from the kid himself. Being the pitcher is awfully exciting, so your child might practice way more than he should to be the top pitcher on the team. Don't let your husband, who's convinced the next Nolan Ryan eats at your dinner table, go out to "play a little catch" in the backyard every night. A little practice is obviously a good thing, but keep an eye on the length and frequency of practice.

WHEN THE DIAMOND IS A GIRL'S BEST FRIEND

Many girls start off in tee-ball and Little League, but are soon directed to softball. *Softball* is very similar to baseball; the main difference is the size of the infield (it's smaller, with only 60 feet between the bases) and the size of the ball (which is bigger). The ball is also not as hard and doesn't travel as far or as fast.

Games are played to seven innings rather than nine, and the only other big difference is that the softball pitch is an underhand pitch. This pitch, however, varies widely, depending on the type of softball a player is playing.

Slow Pitch

In *slow pitch softball*, the pitch is tossed almost gently toward the plate, with an arc between two and ten feet. There's no base stealing in slow pitch ball because it would be so ridiculously easy. Slow pitch teams also have 10 fielders, rather than nine, and 10 batters. The extra fielder is called a *short fielder*, who plays right behind second base.

Fast Pitch

In *fast pitch softball*, the rules are basically identical to baseball. The pitch is underhand, but can still be thrown over the plate at tremendous speeds. The only other thing that differs from baseball is the lead off the base before the ball is hit. In baseball, as long as the runner goes back to the base after each pitch, she can stay off it. In softball, the runner must be on the base until the ball leaves the pitcher's hand. The runner can steal at that point, but she doesn't get to have a lead.

VACANT LOT GAMES

Baseball has spawned more pick-up games than any other sport has. Part of the reason is its elevated status as the national pastime; scores of young boys couldn't imagine playing anything else. There are a million variations, but here's one of the best.

Home Run Derby

Home Run Derby is good with only two players, but it can be played with more, too. In two-player Home Run Derby, one player pitches and the other bats. An area should be marked off as the home run area. A fence is always good, but sticks or sweatshirts can mark off a line, too. Each time the batter hits the ball into the home run area, it counts as a run; any other hit is an out. Three strikes count as an out, too. As in regular baseball, half an inning is over after three outs, and the players switch positions. The player with the most runs after nine innings is the winner.

If there are three players, the inning is divided into three parts instead of two, and the third player shags the fly balls.

With four or more players, the kids should divide into two teams. The batters alternate every time at bat.

LEARNING THE LINGO

The rules of baseball are complicated enough; you don't want the added burden of being lost in the language of the sport, too. The following table has most of the terms you'll hear in your stint as a baseball mom.

Baseball lingo

TERM	EXPLANATION
at bat	A turn up at the plate.
balk	When a pitcher stops her pitching motion without delivering the pitch.
ball	A pitch that's not over the plate or between the batter's knees and shoulders, which isn't swung at by the batter.
base	One of the four corners of the diamond, where a batter is safe from being tagged by the ball.
base path	The dirt area between the bases.
batter	The player trying to hit the pitch.
batting average	The number of at bats a player has had, divided by the number of successful hits.
bunt	A hit in which the batter spreads his hands on the bat and pushes the bat toward the ball instead of swinging at it.
catcher	The position behind the plate.
diamond	The infield.
double play	When a team gets two outs during one at bat.
dugout	The bench area where a team sits when it's not in the field.
ERA	Earned run average.
fair ball	A ball hit within the foul lines.
first baseman	The player covering the area around first base.

TERM	EXPLANATION
force play	When a player must run to the next base. In this case, only the base needs to be tagged, not the runner, to make an out.
foul ball	A ball that's hit outside the foul lines.
foul lines	The lines that lead from home plate past first and third bases and into the outfield.
fly ball	A ball hit into the air in the outfield.
glove	The leather device worn on the hand to help the fielder catch the ball.
grounder	A ball hit along the ground.
home	The plate.
home plate	A rubber pentagon that determines where the pitch must be thrown.
home run	A hit that allows the player to go all the way around the bases in one turn without getting out.
infield	The area outlined by the bases and base paths.
infield fly rule	A rule that says if a ball is hit in the air in the infield with less than two outs and there are runners on base, then it's an automatic out for the batter whether or not the ball is caught.
inning	A unit of play consisting of six outs, three by each team. A baseball game has nine innings; a softball game has seven.
mitt	Another name for a glove.
out	When the fielders stop the batter or runner from reaching a base.

continues

TERM	EXPLANATION
outfield	The grassy area beyond the infield.
outfielder	One of three players covering the outfield.
pitch	The throw to the batter.
pitcher	The player who throws the ball to the batter.
pitcher's mound	The area where the pitcher stands when she delivers the pitch.
pop-up	A short fly ball.
RBI	Stands for runs batted in.
run	The unit of scoring in baseball. Occurs when a player has tagged all three bases and home plate safely.
sacrifice fly	Hitting the ball in the air to the outfield so that a runner can tag up and score.
second baseman	The fielder covering the area between second and first.
short fielder	The tenth player in slow-pitch softball. She is positioned behind second base.
shortstop	The fielder covering the area between third and second base.
stealing	Running to the next base at some time other than during a hit.
strike	A good pitch that was swung at but not hit.
strike out	To miss three good pitches during an at bat.
tee-ball	The first kind of baseball most kids play; the ball is propped up on a tee rather than pitched.

TERM	EXPLANATION
tag up	Waiting until a fly ball is caught and then trying to run to the next base or home before the throw gets there.
third baseman	The fielder guarding the area near third base.
triple play	When a team gets three outs during one at bat.
umpire	The official running the game.
walk	When a batter receives four unacceptable pitches from the pitcher. He gets to go to first base.

It takes so long to learn all the nuances of baseball that you'll end up being a fan for life, just to make the effort pay off. It's probably how baseball became America's pastime.

THE LEAST YOU NEED TO KNOW

◆ Baseball is played on a two-part field: the diamond (or infield) and the outfield.

◆ There are nine players on a team, and each team takes a turn out in the field and up to bat for each of the nine innings.

◆ Batters try to "hit 'em where they ain't."

◆ Fielders try to get the batter out by catching the ball, tagging a base, or tagging the runner.

◆ Softball is similar to baseball.

◆ Little League elbow is a real danger, so baseball moms need to be on the lookout for it.

Tennis Anyone?

Tennis has gone from the sport of the aristocracy to the sport of the masses. It's played at camps, at clubs, and in neighborhoods. Public courts can be found in nearly every city and suburb in the country. It's one of those "lifetime" sports; players' ages range from three to ninety-three.

Whether your child has picked up the game at a camp or a club, you can be pretty sure she'll be playing it for a long time to come. It would be good for you to start learning the game now, before she starts talking about her USTA ranking.

The court, the scoring, and the endless guidelines on game behavior are covered in this chapter. The game itself is explained, too, but it's so simple you really don't need a book to catch on—until you want to know the score, of course.

ALLEYS, END LINES, AND SERVING BOXES

The tennis court is a rectangle, 78 feet long and 36 feet wide, bisected by a three-foot-high net. Running along the sides of the court are two *alleys*; each is four-and-a-half feet wide. The alleys are used only in doubles, which means a singles court is really 78' by 27'.

There are two other lines on the court, shown in the following diagram. Twenty-one feet out from the net is a line that stretches from alley to alley. A center line running perpendicular to that line divides the area in half, creating two *service boxes*. The serve must bounce in one of these two boxes, depending on where the server is standing. The center line doesn't continue all the way back to the baseline, but a small hashmark indicates where it would be.

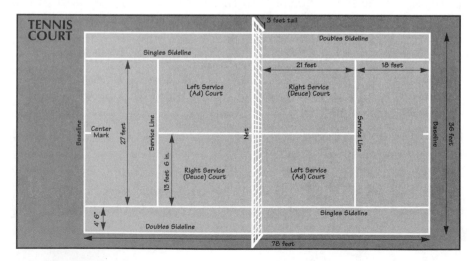

The tennis court.

ONE BIG RACKET

If your child is interested in tennis, he's going to need a racket. Rackets come in many sizes to suit a variety of players. There are three parts to the racket—the *grip* (where you hold the racket), the *throat* (the connecting piece of the handle), and the *head* (where the strings are)—that can all be changed to fit the size and skills of the player.

When buying your child's first racket, your best bet is to go to a tennis club. A pro there can accurately determine what size grip your child should have. If that's not an option, or the prices at your local club are outrageous, you can do it yourself. Have him grip a racket in his hand. His fingers should almost reach the fleshy part of the hand that's below the thumb, and the thumb should overlap the fingers.

As for as the racket's throat and head, this is a good rule for younger players: The smaller the child, the smaller the racket. When your child gets older and more skilled, however, you might want to consider an oversized head (even if he's still small.) A larger racket head gives the player more power, but it does sacrifice some control. You'll have to see what your child likes. If you belong to a club, you can usually try out a racket without buying it.

WHEN LOVE MEANS NOTHING

The scoring in tennis is probably the hardest aspect of the sport. Trying to understand tennis scoring might make you feel like you're opening one of those Russian dolls; every time you remove the top part, there's yet another smaller part underneath it. If you look at a tennis *tournament* as the biggest doll, you'll begin to have a handle on the sport. Inside tournaments are *matches*, inside matches are *sets*, inside sets are *games*, and inside games are *points*.

I'll start with points, the smallest yet most confusing aspect of scoring. Essentially, you need four points to win a game, but you need to win by two. So if you reach 4-1, you win. If you reach 3-3, then you'll have to win at 5-3, and if it goes to 4-4 instead, then you'll have to win at 6-4, and so forth. That part of scoring isn't too difficult.

The problem is that tennis doesn't use the old familiar counting method of 0, 1, 2, 3, 4. No, that would be too easy. In tennis, it's *Love-15-30-40-Game*. *Love* is zero, *15* is your first point, *30* is your second point, *40* your third, and *Game* your fourth. Is that nuts or what? There isn't even a pattern to the numbers—and don't ask me why the first point is called "love."

As if that numbering scheme weren't enough, you still have to deal with the issue of winning by two. Rather than add more crazy numbers, tennis adds only two more crazy terms. A score of 40-40 is called *deuce*. Whoever wins the next point has the *advantage*. In professional tournaments, the announcer says "Advantage Sampras," for instance. In your children's matches, you're more likely to hear the abbreviated "ad in" or "ad out." *Ad in* means that the advantage is the server's, and *ad out* means that the advantage is to the receiver. (You might also hear "my ad" and "your ad," which is even more informal.)

If the person with the advantage doesn't win the point, the score goes back to deuce. This can continue on forever until one person scores two in a row, thus earning the advantage point and the game point. That person then wins the game.

Which brings us to games... Games, fortunately, are counted in the normal way: 1, 2, 3, and so on. The first player (or team, if it's doubles) to reach six games, winning (again) by two, is the winner of the set. If the set reaches 6-6, people usually play a tiebreaker to settle the match. (If it's not an official match or tournament, players may choose to play on until someone wins the set by two games.)

> **TAKING A CLOSER LOOK**
>
> A *tiebreaker* can be done in several ways, but the most common is the 12-point tiebreaker. The server starts in the *deuce court* (the right side) and serves one serve. Then the other person serves two serves, starting with the *ad court* (the left side). Then it's back to the first for two serves until someone reaches seven points (best of 12), winning by two.

Sets are even easier. In most matches, the first player to win two sets is the winner, which means three sets are the maximum that two people (or teams) will play. In men's professional tennis, they play five sets.

After winning two sets, a player has won a match. Unless your child is in a tournament, that's the end of the line. It's hard to say how many matches make up a tournament because the number varies.

PLAY BY THE RULES

"So get on with it," you're saying. "I'm well into the chapter, and I don't even know how to start yet."

To begin, there are two ways to play tennis: singles and doubles. If I try to explain the doubles and singles game at the same time, we're both going to lose it, so for now I'll just cover the singles rules and move on to doubles later in the chapter.

Serve It Up

The game begins with a serve. The serving player always begins behind the baseline, somewhere to the right of the hashmark that divides the court in half. She tosses the ball into the air with her hand and bats it with the racket into the service box on her opponent's right side. In other words, she hits it diagonally. The ball may not hit the net or bounce on the server's side of the court.

The server may not step on or over the baseline at any point before the serve, but she may cross it the moment after the ball has been struck by the racket. That's when the serve is officially over.

She doesn't have to wait until it gets to the other side. If the ball has already been hit, the step is legal.

If the server misses in some way, it's called a *fault*, and she gets one more try. Two misses in a row is called a *double fault*, and the point goes to the receiver. If the ball hits the net, but still manages to go into the service box, it's called a *let*, which essentially means "do over."

Rally Ho!

After the ball bounces into the service box, the opponent hits it back over the net. It can land anywhere between the alleys and the baseline. This batting back and forth is called a *rally* and continues until someone hits the ball outside the court's boundaries or into the net or fails to get to the ball within one bounce. When any one of these things happens, the point is over.

After the first point, the server moves to the left side of the court for her serve. She continues alternating sides for each new point. When the game is over, it's the other player's turn to serve.

Here are a few more tidbits about rallying:

◆ Lines are considered part of the court, so a ball is still in if it bounces on the line.

◆ After each odd game (first, third, fifth, and so on), the players switch sides. This change helps reduce the effect that sun or wind might have on an outdoor game.

◆ A player must let the ball bounce on the serve. Every other time, he's allowed to hit the ball while it's in the air.

◆ A player may reach over the net to hit a ball but may never touch the net.

For the spectator, a good rally is the most gratifying part of tennis. The tension builds with each hit. Is this the end? Is this the last point? Will he get to that shot? Can she put this one away? Unless you're someone who loves to gab in the bleachers, you'll love being a tennis mom.

INSTANT REPLAY

In one match I was watching, the player I was rooting for, a young girl named Martha, hit a drop shot over the net, with a tremendous amount of spin on it. It took one bounce onto her opponent's court and then spun back into Martha's court without her opponent touching it. The match ground to a halt. Whose point was it? Did Martha get the point because her opponent never hit the ball? Or did the opponent get the point because the ball was returned to Martha's court, even though it did it without help? A quick call was placed to the United States Tennis Association (USTA). The verdict: Martha's point. If that situation ever comes up again, you should know that it's legal for the opponent to have reached over the net to hit the ball on Martha's side.

DOUBLE YOUR FUN

Doubles tennis is a variation on singles tennis. Rather than one against one, it's two against two. Because there are more players on the court, the court conveniently gets wider, so now the alleys are part of the playing area.

Players on a team choose which side of the court will be theirs to cover. The right side is referred to as the *forehand court* or *deuce court*, and the left side is the *backhand court* or *ad court*. This terminology is relevant only for the serves, however. Players can switch back and forth at any other time. At the beginning of each new set, they can choose to switch.

The server begins on the right-hand side, as in singles. Although the alleys are in use for the game, the serve still must land within the singles serving box. The receiver of the first serve is the player in the forehand court.

At the second serve, the server moves to the left side, and her partner, who is usually up at the net, moves to the right side. One person serves an entire game. The receiver is now the player on the backhand court. She, most likely, was at the net in the previous point, so she will move back to receive while her partner moves up to the net. Everything happens in the reverse for the next point.

The second game is served by the forehand court player on the other team. The third game is served by the backhand court player on the first team, and the fourth game is served by the last player. Even when the backhand court players are the servers, the serve begins on the right side of the court.

All the other rules for doubles are the same as singles. The scoring is the same, and the teams still switch sides after every odd game. However, even though the rules are the same, doubles somehow ends up being quite a different game. The strategy is much different, and communication is key. There are way too many stories of doubles partners beaning each other with the ball or whacking each other with rackets. I'm assuming most of those bruisings are accidental, stemming from both players' eager desire to go for the ball.

INSTANT REPLAY

 There's a pairing in the doubles game called *mixed doubles*. It might as well be called "double trouble." In mixed doubles, there's a male and female on each team, and more often than not, it ends up being a husband and wife team.

At one club, the club tennis champion was a man whose wife was just getting into the game. He urged her to join him in the mixed doubles tournament "just for fun. No pressure." She agreed, and lo and behold, they won their first two matches. It was looking as though they might have a chance to win, so it was no longer just for fun. The husband instructed the wife to remain in the alley and not touch the ball unless it came right at her. He then played essentially a singles game. The two of them lost at that point, though, and the wife, humiliated, has refused to play mixed doubles with her husband ever since.

A SPORT FOR MISS MANNERS

Tennis has long had a reputation as an elitist sport—the sport of country clubs. Players had to wear crisp white outfits, with skirts for women and collared shirts for men. The t-shirted masses weren't allowed. On top of that, everyone's behavior was always very proper.

Well, things have changed somewhat. Tennis is available to almost everyone now, and public courts don't require the white uniform. Many country clubs have "relaxed" the rules a bit too, making the bold move of allowing their players to wear a colored top or bottom (not both). The tennis code of conduct, however, is still in effect. If you want every detail, the USTA actually sells a book called *The Code*, but I'll give you an overview in the following sections.

In the Bleachers

When you're watching your child play tennis, you're expected to be a very different type of fan than the mom watching her son on the line in football or her daughter pitch in softball. There's no yelling "Crush him!" or "No batter, no batter. Hum it in there!"

Tennis fans are quiet. During a point, ideally there should be complete silence on the court. After a point has been won, there's controlled clapping…and that's about it. Are you still surprised that tennis was once thought of as a sport for only the uptight and reserved?

A-Courting We Will Go

The Code on the court is very similar. You aren't allowed to yell or distract your opponents. If you have any doubt that the ball might be out (or in), you must give the call to your opponents. You may not sulk, stall, or complain. My personal favorite is this rule:

"Players are expected to maintain full control over their emotions and the resulting behavior throughout the match. If you begin to lose your composure during play, try the following:

◆ Take several deep breaths, exhale as slowly as possible, and feel your muscles relax.

◆ Concentrate on your own game and behavior while ignoring distractions from your opponent or surroundings.

◆ Be your own best friend—enjoy your good shots and forget the poor ones."

Wouldn't you just love to have your children live on a tennis court?

COUNTRY CLUB CAPERS

The beauty of tennis is that it can be played with only two people. You don't have to round up a team or invent new variations on the game the way you do in other sports when players are in short supply. Nevertheless, there are still some variations your child might want to play.

Twenty-One

The basics of *Twenty-One* are similar to regular tennis, but the scoring is different. (Thank goodness, right?) It gets players to rush to the net more often, which is a good habit for a player to get into.

The game begins with a serve. For every winning shot from the baseline, the player scores one point. For every winning shot from the net, the player scores two points. The first player to reach 21 points wins. Besides being a fun game, it's also a quick lesson in when it's appropriate to rush the net and when it's not.

Popcorn

If you don't have a court to practice on, *Popcorn* is a good game to play. It's fun and it helps develop eye-hand coordination and racket control. It's good for three or more players.

Everyone spreads out in a large circle. The first player hits the ball off her racket up into the air to the next player. That person must hit it to the player next to him. All this must be done without the ball touching the ground. If it does, then the player who misses is eliminated. (The group has to decide whether it was the hitter or the receiver who made the error.) Play continues until only one player, the winner, is left.

LEARNING THE LINGO

If your child's tennis is going to be played at a country club, it's time you learned to talk the talk. It will probably come in handy in other places, too. The following table covers the pertinent points of tennis lingo.

Tennis lingo	
TERM	*EXPLANATION*
ace	A serve that completely blows by the opponent.
ad court	The left side of the court.
ad in	When the server is ahead by one. This can happen only after the players have already reached deuce.
ad out	When the receiver is ahead by one. This can happen only after the players have already reached deuce.
advantage	One person is leading by one point after at least seven points have been played.
alley	The sides of the court, which are used only in doubles.
backhand court	The left side of the court.
breaking a serve	Someone beats his opponent when the opponent is the one serving.
deuce	The score is tied at three or more points each.
deuce court	The right side of the court.
double fault	Two missed serves in a row, resulting in a lost point.
doubles	Two players play against two other players.
drop shot	A short shot with a lot of spin that barely makes it over the net. Used mostly when the other player is way back at the baseline.
fault	A missed serve.
forehand court	The right side of the court.

continues

Tennis lingo *continued*

TERM	*EXPLANATION*
let	A do-over.
lob	A high looping shot used when the other player has rushed the net. This gets the ball over his head and forces him back.
love	The score of zero.
mixed doubles	A male and female team play against another male and female team.
rally	A series of hits.
service box	The area that the serve must bounce into.
singles	One player plays against one other player.
volley	Hitting a shot while it's in the air; the ball doesn't bounce on the court.

The beauty of tennis is that it can be played at age 3 or age 93. It's a lifetime sport that isn't dependent on a team, a school, or even the weather, now that there are so many indoor facilities. Children shouldn't be pushed into playing a sport, but tennis is one that has a good run for its money.

THE LEAST YOU NEED TO KNOW

- ◆ Tennis is played on a tennis court between two people or between two teams of two people each.
- ◆ Tournaments are made up of matches, which are made up of sets, which are made up of games, which are made up of points.
- ◆ Plays begins with a serve, and a point ends when one player either hits the ball into the net or out of the court.
- ◆ Manners are a big deal in this sport.

Golf Galore

You can't open a sports page without seeing some mention of Tiger Woods. His phenomenal accomplishments have made golf the hot "new" sport. His name is on everyone's lips, and parents are getting their kids on the links as young as three, hoping their cubs will turn into Tigers, too.

Your child is jumping on the bandwagon, too, and you're wondering if you should support him. Is it worth it? Absolutely! Golf is a great sport, no matter what your level of play. The four-hour walk that an 18-hole course usually requires is great exercise, eye-hand coordination is challenged, and except for an errant ball here and there, it's one of the safest sports a person can play.

There are a couple of drawbacks, however. The cost can be prohibitive, and the time demands are considerable. On top of that, golf is not perfect for every personality. In golf, you know exactly how well you performed at the end of the course because you have your score. While you're learning the game, your score goes down every time you play; however, at some point you plateau, which can drive certain golfers crazy.

This chapter describes a typical golf course in terms more detailed but less eloquent than Mark Twain's effort; he called golf "a good walk spoiled." The course is pretty, but it can also be pretty aggravating. The equipment has complications all its own, so a good portion of this chapter is devoted to explaining what your child will need. Finally, the actual play is addressed. After that comes a brief etiquette lesson, an explanation of handicaps, and a few other games to liven up the sport.

BET YOU DIDN'T KNOW

Golf is generally thought to have originated in Scotland. The country certainly deserves some credit for having made golf a popular sport worldwide. It boasts some of the best courses in the world and has some of the most devoted players. In fact, in the fifteenth century, the Scots were forbidden to play the game because it was taking too much time away from archery practice!

OF COURSE!

Golf is played on a golf *course*. Although every course is different, all courses have the same components. They are either 18 holes (which is the standard) or 9 holes long, with each hole being about 200 to 600 yards long. If you play all the holes in the course, you have played a *round* of golf.

The shortest holes are *par 3* holes, which means that a good golfer could get the ball in the cup in three strokes. There are usually about four of them on an eighteen-hole course. The longest holes are *par 5*, and a course typically has four of them, too. The other ten holes are all par 4s.

Each of the holes has a *tee box*, a *fairway*, a *rough*, and a *green*. Some holes have *water traps*, and some have *sand traps*. Some holes are extra long, and some just have a whole lot of trees lining the *fairway*. A typical hole is shown in the following figure.

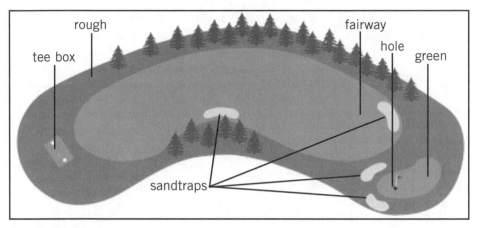

A typical hole.

TAKING A CLOSER LOOK

You might have heard golfers referring to the 19th hole. Look out if you hear your child talking about it. The 19th hole is the "watering hole" back in the club's bar.

The *tee box* (also called the *teeing ground* or just plain *tee*) is a grassy flat area at the start of a hole. On standard courses, the tee box is usually bracketed by three different color markers. The colors vary from club to club, but most use red, white, and blue. The red markers indicate where women start the hole, the white are for men, and the blue are for pros.

The tee box is the only area on a hole where the golfer may touch the ball. He places the ball on a small wooden device called a *tee*. The tee props the ball up off the ground, which makes it easier for the golfer to hit. It was probably invented because golfers like their first shot, which is usually made in front of the onlookers in the clubhouse, to be a good one.

The *fairway* is the beautiful green carpet leading up to the flag at the end of the hole. In this perfectly groomed area, it's relatively easy to hit a good shot. Every golfer would ideally like to hit off the tee and land in the fairway.

Sometimes, though, the ball *hooks* (goes to the left), *slices* (goes to the right), or *dribbles* (doesn't go in the air—also called a *worm-burner*) off the tee and lands in the weedy, unkempt area of the hole called the *rough*. It's a little harder to hit from there.

BET YOU DIDN'T KNOW

Before the wooden tee was invented, golfers perched their balls on little piles of wet sand. Buckets of sand were kept at the tee box for this purpose.

Beyond the rough, however, lies even more danger. Woods, water, and sand torment golfers at every turn. These areas are called *hazards* and are added to a hole to make the game more difficult.

Finally, at the end of the hole lies the *green*, or *putting green*, as it's sometimes called. It's a finely mowed area with a hole, called the *cup*, somewhere within its boundaries. (The cup is moved periodically to different parts of the green.) A flag sticks out of the cup to let golfers know where the actual hole is when they're approaching the green. Surrounding the green is about two feet of slightly longer grass called the *apron*.

CLUBS AND A CLUB

Golf isn't a bargain sport. In terms of cost, it's almost tied with skiing, and perhaps ice hockey, as the most expensive (mainstream) sport around.

Club Hopping

To begin with, you need a place to play. At the cheapest end are the par 3 public courses. They are nine-hole courses, and each hole is short (a par 3). They're relatively inexpensive; one I know of, for example, charges $15 for a season membership and $2.50 each time you play—and it's even cheaper for kids.

Next, there are eighteen-hole public courses, which cost between $20 and $200 a round, depending on where you want to play. At the highest end of the spectrum are the private clubs. Some charge an annual fee, which can run anywhere from $3,000 to

$25,000. Others have a one-time bond or initiation fee, too, and that can run from $10,000 to $100,000. Still want your child taking up the sport?

The good news is that golf's popularity is exploding. Something like 800 new courses were built in this country last year, with another 800 slated to be built in the next few years. With this glut of new courses, there ought to be one in your price range.

If the local high school has a team, and your child gets on it, the fees won't be an issue. Some private schools have their own courses, and the public ones usually get time donated to them by a local course.

Clubs for the Club

The next big ticket item is equipment. Like the huge disparity in course prices, the clubs you need can cost anywhere from $30 for a used set to $2,500 for a full set of state-of-the-art clubs.

Fourteen clubs are all that's allowed on the course at one time, so a full set would probably include three *woods*, ten *irons*, and a *putter*.

Despite their name, woods are no longer made of wood. The *1 wood* is usually called a *driver* because it's what you use to drive the ball off the tee. There's not much slant to the club's head, which is quite big. Some beginning golfers have trouble using the 1 wood.

The *3 wood* has more of a slant, and the head is a little narrower. These features make it easier for inexperienced players to use the 3 wood as a driver. The *5 wood* is more slanted than the 3 wood and is even used on the fairway. In fact, it's often referred to as a *fairway wood*.

The irons range in number from 1 to 9, with 1 being the least slanted and 9 being the most slanted. Irons get shorter as they go up in number, so the lower the number, the longer the shot and the lower the *loft*, the arc in the air. The distance from the hole determines which iron a player uses. The irons include the *sand wedge* (used in sand traps) and the *pitching wedge*, which is even more lofted than the 9 iron and is used for *chipping* (short, lofted shots) near the green.

Finally, the *putter* is used for hitting the ball on the ground when it's on the green.

TAKING A CLOSER LOOK

A club called the baffler is used to hit shots in the rough. It has ridges on the bottom, which allows a player to get down lower in the grass to get underneath the ball without getting the club head caught in the grass.

Frankly, until your child is good at golf, she's not going to need every single club. She certainly won't know the difference between her shot with a 6 iron and her shot with a 5 iron. You might consider getting her just a putter, the 3 wood, and the odd-numbered irons to save money. A local sports store can point you in the right direction. Just make sure that kids get children's clubs, and teen-age girls get women's clubs. Teen-age boys should get regular men's clubs.

You need a bag, balls, shoes, and tees, too, but those items are all negligible in cost by comparison. Did I ask if you still want your kid to play the sport?

DIFFERENT STROKES

The object of golf is to complete the course in fewer strokes than your opponent. To progress through the course, a player must hit his ball from the tee box (called a *drive*) and use one or more strokes to get the ball into the cup at the end of the hole.

From Start to Finish

To start, the ball is placed on the tee. If it falls off before the player swings at it, it's considered an embarrassing little incident that doesn't count as a stroke. If the player swings and misses and the ball stays on the tee, it counts as one stroke. The ball is now in play, so if it's bumped off the tee after the miss, it counts as another stroke and may not be replaced on the tee.

After the ball is hit from the tee, it usually lands in the fairway. The golfer then chooses one of his irons and hits his second shot from there. This continues until the ball lands on the green. When all the players' balls are on the green, the flag is removed from the cup. At this point, the golfers use their putters to lightly tap their balls into the cup. A player should remove his ball after it goes in the cup and before the next player putts.

If the player touches the ball at any time with a club, it counts as a stroke, whether or not he was planning to hit the ball at that moment. And, with the exception of placing the ball on the tee at the start of the hole or removing the ball from a water hazard, the player may not touch the ball with any part of his body until the ball has reached the green. There, the player may pick it up to clean it or to get it out of the way of another player's putt, but he must use some sort of marker to indicate where the ball should be returned.

At the green, items in the line of the putt, such as leaves, sticks, or another player's ball, may be removed. At any other place on the hole, these objects must remain where they are. Artificial objects, however, such as a discarded bottle or a rake, may be removed.

Hazardous Play

Sometimes the ball ends up in the sand trap. Big bummer. Not only does the player have to hit the ball out of the trap, which might have a huge overhang in the direction of the hole, but extra rules can make doing so more difficult. To begin with, a player can't extract a ball that is buried in the sand. She can only brush the sand away slightly so she's able to see a little of the ball.

The golfer must make sure not to touch the sand with her club before she takes her swing. Every time she touches the sand with the club, it counts as a stroke. After the player gets out of the sand trap, she should rake over the sand she disturbed.

BET YOU DIDN'T KNOW

One of the big rules of golf is that you aren't allowed to improve your line of play anywhere except on the green. For instance, you can't move sticks that lie in front of your ball or tree branches that hang down and block your swing. What I find most incredible, however, is that if a sand trap has been left unraked, you aren't allowed to fix it until you're past it, even though it should have been raked before you got there.

Water hazards are a little harder to deal with than sand traps because golfers frequently can't hit the ball out of them. A player might be able to hit the ball out of a trickle of water, but not a deep lake. If a player has to fish his ball out (or get a new one if the lake is deep), he takes a *penalty stroke*, which means adding one more stroke to his score. He can then put the ball back at the point where he took the shot that went into the hazard, or put the ball directly behind the water hazard at the place it went in. Why anyone would ever go back to the first spot is beyond me.

If you lose a ball in the woods or long grass, the options and penalties are the same as with water hazards.

TEE PARTY ETIQUETTE

Like tennis, golf is a sport that's heavy on etiquette. Some etiquette rules, such as checking to make sure no one is standing nearby when you swing, are for safety, but others simply make the experience more pleasant for everyone. Here are the main points of golf etiquette:

- A player who has been in a sand trap should rake over her footprints and ball holes.

- All *divots* (chunks of grass) should be replaced.

- Carts and bags should not be on the green, and care should be taken that the green isn't chewed up.

- The player who got the best score on the last hole (called *honors*) goes first on the next hole.

- No one should talk or move during another player's shot.

- Players should not hit the ball when others are within striking distance.

- If you're playing slowly and the group behind you has to wait, you should wave them through.

- Move quickly through the course. Don't take lots of practice swings or search too long for missing balls if people are waiting.

- The player whose ball is farthest from the hole putts first.

◆ When you're on the green, never cross that imaginary line between a player's ball and the hole.

The list can go on and on, but these 10 guidelines are the most important for beginners to know.

THE BIG PLUS TO HANDICAPS

So now you and your child know everything you wanted to know about golf, but the only person you know who belongs to a club is your father-in-law. Can your son, a beginner, have fun on the course with his grandfather? Absolutely!

Golf is one of those sports in which an experienced player can go out with a novice and both can have fun. The novice might take a little longer getting from tee to cup, but as long as he doesn't take a gazillion practice swings, the time difference shouldn't be enough to bother the other player. The score at the end, however, is going to be quite different, so the game, although enjoyable for both, isn't truly competitive.

This is where the *handicap* comes in, a number determined from previous scores. The player takes the top ten scores from his last 20 rounds of golf and plugs them into a rather complicated equation (a pro golf shop can do this for you). Say this number comes out to be 12. This means that on an average course, you will shoot about 12 strokes over the par for the course.

When you're playing with another player, then, you can each compare handicaps. If yours is 12 and the other player's is 8, you get to subtract four strokes from your score at the end.

If you're playing something called *match play golf*, it's a little more complicated. In match play, you try to win each hole individually. If you win a hole, you get one point for that hole. At the end, the player with the most points wins. In this case, subtracting strokes at the end is useless. They aren't even counted. So in match play, if the difference in handicaps is 4, you subtract one each from the four hardest holes. (The holes are ranked on the scorecard.)

LIVEN UP THE LINKS

Sometimes the golf game needs a bit of modifying for one reason or another. Here are some alternatives.

Speed Golf

Speed Golf is a perfect game for children because they never seem to enjoy the leisurely pace of "adult" golf anyway. In Speed Golf, the score doesn't matter. The object of the game is to get through the course as fast as possible. Of course, the fewer the hits, the faster your pace will be.

Players must wait for the ball to come to a complete rest before they can hit it again. The player to complete a course in the shortest amount of time—regardless of score—is the winner. (It's not a good game to play on busy courses during weekends.)

Target

If you're not on a course, but you still want to play, *Target* is a good game for the backyard. Get a bucket, sandbox, wading pool, or anything else you like and designate it as the target. Each player should have a pile of balls and a club. The object of the game is to chip, or lift, the balls into the target. The player to get the most balls in is the winner.

LEARNING THE LINGO

You don't want to feel out of place at your new country club, so take a look at the terms in the following table to familiarize yourself with the lingo on the links.

Golf lingo	
TERM	*EXPLANATION*
apron	The area of slightly longer grass surrounding the green.
bunker	A sand trap.

TERM	EXPLANATION
caddie	The person who carries a player's clubs around the course, often offering advice.
casual water	Water that isn't supposed to be on the course, so is therefore not a water hazard. You may pick your ball up and take a free drop near it, no closer to the hole.
cup	The actual hole.
divot	A chunk of grass removed by the club during a shot. It should be replaced by the golfer.
drive	The first shot off the tee.
fairway	The groomed area leading up to the green.
"Fore!"	What golfers yell if the ball is heading toward another golfer.
green	The finely mowed area around the hole. Only putting is allowed on the green.
hazard	A water trap or sand trap.
hole	One "unit" in golf, from the tee box to the green.
honors	Winning the previous hole.
hook	A shot that curves to the left (for a right-handed golfer).
irons	Metal clubs with a flat blade on the end.
match play	A game in which the holes won, rather than the strokes, are counted.
mulligan	A do-over, usually off the first tee only. It's illegal, but a common practice during friendly matches.

continues

TERM	*EXPLANATION*
putter	The club used to tap the ball into the hole when you're on the green.
rough	The ungroomed area around the fairway.
slice	A shot that curves to the right (for a right-handed golfer).
tee	A small wooden device that props up the ball.
tee box	The area at the start of the hole.
woods	The clubs, no longer made of wood, that have a block on the end. They are used for long shots.

Golf is a sport that can be fun for the whole family, the athletic-minded, the lazier types (they can ride the carts), the beginners, the experts, the musclemen, and the finesse players. The sport has so many different facets and ways to play that everyone can find something that suits.

THE LEAST YOU NEED TO KNOW

◆ Golf is a safe, challenging sport for kids. Unfortunately it requires lots of time and money.

◆ The object of golf is to complete the course in fewer strokes than an opponent.

◆ Basic golf etiquette requires that a player does not interrupt or obstruct another's game.

7

Lacrosse Examination

Lacrosse is one of the greatest sports imaginable for an athlete. It takes tremendous skill and stamina and is incredibly exciting with nonstop action. For a mom, it's the ultimate sports nightmare.

It's not a professional sport, so you can't immerse yourself in television games, hoping to learn something through osmosis, and it's not a sport you might have grown up with. Until recently, lacrosse was a sport confined to a few Northeastern private schools. Now it's spreading rapidly to other parts of the country, too. No matter how widespread it gets, however, it will always be confusing. I was talking to the father of my local high school's lacrosse team captain, and he still needs help with the rules.

There's one more thing that will really get you. The girls' game and the boys' game are about as similar as a pair of third cousins twice removed.

This chapter covers the field, the positions, and the rules for both the boys' and girls' games. It also suggests some games to play that can be used by either boys or girls. Finally, it wraps up with a lacrosse language lesson.

> ### BET YOU DIDN'T KNOW
>
> Lacrosse was first invented by Native Americans. They used it as both a game and a way of improving hunting and warrior skills. Called *baggataway*, it was played all year long, regardless of weather conditions. The rules weren't rigid, and sometimes hundreds of players would play at once. The French Canadians referred to it as *la crosse* because that's what they called the stick the Native Americans used.

FOR BOYS ONLY

Many football players gravitate to lacrosse because both games share a similar type of attack mentality. Given that lacrosse originated as a sort of practice war game, this isn't surprising.

Play the Field

The boys' game of lacrosse is played on a field that's 110 yards by 60–70 yards. A *midfield line* divides the field in half. The goals aren't on the edges of the field; rather, they're 15 yards in from the *end line*, so play can take place behind the goal. There are 80 yards between the two goals; each has a 6 foot by 6 foot opening.

A circle, nine feet in diameter, around each goal is called the *crease*. Only the goalkeeper is allowed within the crease. Twenty yards out in front of each goal is a line that marks the *goal area*. This goal area is 40 yards across the top and 35 yards on the sides. On each side of the field, bisected by the midfield line, is a 20-yard-long line that's 20 yards away from the center of the field. It marks the *wing area*.

Oddly enough, most of these markings are used only when play begins, at the start of a quarter or after a goal.

Pick Up Sticks

To play, each player needs a lacrosse stick. In fact, unless they have one hand on their stick, they aren't allowed to be involved in the play, even if they're going to kick the ball. The lacrosse stick is officially called a *crosse*, although many players just refer to it as their *stick*. The crosse is a long plastic stick with a semi-triangular net, called a *basket*, on the end. Players like to create a pocket in their basket to hold the ball, but the rule book says it can't be so deep that the ball sits below the plastic.

> ### BET YOU DIDN'T KNOW
>
> The boys' lacrosse stick has undergone some dramatic changes over the years. Originally, lacrosse sticks were made of wood and the basket was made of leather. Only one side of the basket was rimmed with wood. Now the sticks are made of plastic and aluminum with a nylon basket and the rim (or *wall*) goes all the way around. Plastic has some advantages because wooden sticks broke all the time, and new baskets had to be broken in.

There are three types of crosses. The *goalie's crosse* is short, but it has a basket that's about a foot wide, which helps with blocking. There can be only one goalie's stick on the field at a time. The *attack stick* (for offensive players) is also short, but it has a very skinny basket, which helps hold the ball. The *defense stick* is long, so defensive players can reach far to intercept the balls. Its basket is smaller than the goalie's stick but larger than the attack stick.

Also included on the equipment list are cleats, a helmet with a face guard, shoulder pads, elbow pads, and heavy protective gloves. All this protective gear is necessary because whacking another player's stick, called *checking*, is totally acceptable in boy's lacrosse. The rules state that the arm is an extension of the stick and therefore may be checked with impunity. Ow! Who thought of that rule?

The goalkeeper also adds a chest pad, thigh pads, and shin guards.

Game Time

The object of lacrosse is to score more goals than the other team in the time allotted for play. This time varies depending on the level of play, ranging from 36 minutes to 60 minutes. The game is divided into four quarters. In case of a tie, the amount of overtime is also determined by the level of play.

The Players

There are 10 players on a team: three *attack* players, three *midfielders* (who play both attack and defense), three *defensive* players, and one *goalie*. At the start of the game, the attack players must be in the goal area in front of the opponent's goal. The midfielders are in the middle of the field, with one in each wing area and one in the center. The defensive players are in the goal area in front of their own goal.

TAKING A CLOSER LOOK

Each position has a name, although the names aren't commonly used anymore. The three attack players are called the *first attack*, the *out home*, and the *in home*. The midfielders are *center*, *second defense*, and *second attack*, and the defensive players are *point*, *cover point*, and *first defense*.

Substitutions can happen at any time; the players can run on and off the field without stopping play. However, more than 10 players aren't allowed on the field at once, so the sub has to wait for the player on the field to be fully off before going on.

The Face-Off

At the beginning of each quarter and after a goal, the play starts with a *face-off* (or *face*) in the center of the field. This means that two opposing players trap the ball between the backs of their crosses, while the crosses are completely on the ground. At the referee's whistle each player tries to gain control of the ball or get it to a teammate. As the two centers are battling, the wing midfielders are allowed to move out of the wing area, but the other players aren't allowed to move out of the goal areas until one team gains clear possession of the ball.

Moving the Ball

After the face-off, the players may go anywhere they want. However, three of the team's players must remain on the attack half of the field and four of the team's players (including the goalie) must stay on the field's defending side. For instance, if a defender has the ball and wants to run with it, a midfielder must remain on the defensive end until the regular defense player returns.

No one is allowed to touch the lacrosse ball with his hands except for the goalkeeper, who may do so only to prevent a ball from going in the goal. He's not allowed to catch the ball or throw it.

To move the ball down the field, players may run with it in their crosse (called *cradling* it), pass it to another player, or kick it. They can also bat the ball along the ground, using their stick like a hockey stick.

The defensive players try to intercept the ball or knock the ball out of the attack players' sticks by *poke-checking* (whacking the other person with the stick) or by *body-checking* (bumping them with the body). Even if a player doesn't have a ball, he can be body-checked, as long as he's within five yards of the ball—way too tempting for young boys.

Both attack and defense are allowed to physically try to keep the opponent from getting the ball or moving toward it as long as they're pushing against the player while keeping both hands on the stick.

Out of Bounds

If the ball goes out of bounds while it's being moved down the field, then it goes to the team opposing the team who last touched it. If, however, the ball goes out after a shot, then the closest player to the ball as it goes over the line gets the ball back.

During a youth league lacrosse game, one goalkeeper was pretty bored. His team was dominating the game, and the ball just wasn't making it to his end of the field. To burn off all this energy he wasn't using, he kicked grass, jumped up and down, hit the goal posts with his stick, and finally kicked the net. Big mistake. His cleat got caught in the netting. He gave it a yank, but it was stuck. He turned to see if he had time to get it out, and wouldn't you know it, the other team was heading straight for him! He panicked, pulled more, and ended up standing on one foot, crying, as the other team scored its only goal of the day.

Fouls on the Field

There are two kinds of fouls in lacrosse: *personal* and *technical*. Personal fouls include the following:

◆ Body-checking below the knees

◆ Body-checking from behind

◆ Body-checking when the player isn't within five yards of the ball

◆ Tripping

◆ *Slashing* (swinging the stick at any part of the opponent except for the arm)

◆ *Crosse-checking* (hitting the opponent with the shaft of the stick that's between the hands)

◆ Unsportsmanlike behavior

A player who commits a personal foul must leave the game for one or three minutes, depending on the severity of the foul. The team cannot replace him and must play short a man. If, however, there's a face-off during this time, they may choose which position to leave empty, even if the player played a different position.

Technical fouls are called when a player does something illegal but not injurious. Here are the technical fouls:

- Touching the ball with the hand (except for the goalie)

- Offside, which happens when there aren't four defense players (one being the goalkeeper) on the defensive side of the midfield line or three attack players on the attack side of the midfield line

- Stepping in the crease, which may be occupied only by the goalie

- Warding off another player by pushing him away with an arm

- Holding onto a player or his stick

The penalties for technical fouls are either losing the ball (if the offender had possession at the time of the foul) or sitting out for 30 seconds, if the fouled player had possession.

If the coach gets thrown out of the game for some reason, such as yelling at the referee, then one of his team's attacking players must sit out for three minutes. Any player who commits five personal fouls in one game will be ejected, too, with the same results for the team.

FOR GIRLS ONLY

The girls' game is a more graceful game than the boys' because the players aren't allowed to whack at each other or collide into one another. Nonetheless, it still has its fair share of injuries. I know of one girl who had to go to her prom with a black eye from a ball that bounced off her crosse into her face.

BET YOU DIDN'T KNOW

Men's lacrosse began in North America, but the women's game began in England. A team from Canada was visiting England and demonstrated the game for the Queen. Some women gym teachers introduced it to the private school circuit with several rule variations, making it more gentle.

Natural Boundaries

The field in girls' lacrosse is a little hard to define because technically it has no boundaries. Natural—or somewhat unnatural, for that matter—boundaries such as woods, a drainage ditch, a fence, bleachers, or a grandmother in a lawn chair create the edges of the field.

The only markings on the field are a *center circle* (with a 10-yard radius) and two circles around the goals. The area around the goal is called the *crease*, just as in the boys' game, but the crease in the girls' game is a little larger (17 feet in diameter rather than 9). The goals, again with six-foot by six-foot square openings, are ideally 110 yards apart but can be as close as 90 yards apart to allow for plenty of room behind the goal.

A Crosse to Bear

The equipment for girls' lacrosse is minimal. Players wear cleats and a mouthguard and carry a crosse. The girls' lacrosse stick is somewhat different from the boys'. It's made of plastic or wood, and the pocket in the basket is very shallow. It's illegal to have more than half of the ball showing below the rim, so cradling requires much more skill and almost always two hands. In the boys' game, you'll often see players cradling with only one hand.

The goalkeepers are the only players who wear protective equipment. They have a chest protector, thigh protectors, shin guards, gloves, and a helmet with a mask.

Take Your Positions

The object of the game is the same as the boys' game: to score more goals than the opponents in the allotted time. The girls' game, however, is played in two 25-minute halves, and if it's tied, there's no overtime.

There are 12 players on each team.

- ◆ **goalkeeper**   The player protecting the goal and the only player allowed in the crease.

- ◆ **point**   The defensive player who is closest to the goalkeeper.

- ◆ **cover point**   The middle defense player.

- ◆ **third man**   The defensive player who is closest to the center.

- ◆ **right defense wing**   One of the side players.

- ◆ **left defense wing**   One of the side players.

- ◆ **center**   The midfielder who takes the draw.

- ◆ **right attack wing**   One of the side players.

- ◆ **left attack wing**   One of the side players.

- ◆ **third home**   The attacker third in line, closest to the mid-field.

- ◆ **second home**   The second attacker.

- ◆ **first home**   The frontmost attacker.

With the exception of the goalkeeper, there are absolutely no restrictions about where these girls can run on the field.

Each of the positions obviously has an opposite on the other team, and players on defense tightly guard the opposing players on offense. The offense has to make sharp, quick moves and run plays to get open to shoot the ball.

Players can be substituted only at the half, unless the coaches agree otherwise. If they do, then a player taken out in the first half may not go in until the start of the second half.

The Draw

Play begins with a *draw*. The two centers hold their sticks up, trapping the ball between the backs of the crosses. All the other players must remain outside the center circle. At the whistle, the two centers try to gain control or get the ball to a teammate. Once the ball is in play, players move the ball down the field, cradling it while they run or passing it to a teammate. They may not kick it or bat it the way they do in the boys' game.

Foul Play

Fouls are called for rough checking (players are allowed to lightly tap an opponent's stick, but that's it), holding down a player's crosse, reaching across a player's shoulder so she can't move forward, touching the ball with the hands, or guarding the ball with a part of the body.

The ref will also blow the whistle for a violation of the crease. Unlike the boys' game, players may step inside the crease, but only to run through it to get the ball. They may not step into the crease with the ball, receive the ball within the crease, or be caught in it when the ball is being shot by another player. In general, it's probably best for a player to just stay out of the crease.

The goalkeeper is off-limits while she is in the crease, but she may not pull a ball back into the crease to protect it (and herself) unless both her feet are already inside it.

When a foul occurs, the referee blows the whistle and all the players must freeze where they are. The player who was fouled gets a *free position*, which means any player near her is moved at least five yards away, and she gets the ball. She can either shoot it, pass it, or run with it when the referee blows the whistle again.

If the foul was committed in front of the goal, the free position also includes clearing away all the defense players between the fouled player and the goal.

The referee will also blow the whistle when the ball goes into an unplayable area, such as into the woods or over a fence. When this happens, the ref blows the whistle and gives the ball to the player nearest to it. If it's not clear who's closest to the ball, the ref tosses the ball into the air between the two closest players. This is called a *throw*.

TAKING A CLOSER LOOK

The rule requiring players to freeze at the referees' whistle isn't quite as rigid as the freeze rule in Red Light Green Light or Freeze Tag. A player may keep herself moving in her own little spot.

The View from the Bleachers

If there are bleachers at the girls' lacrosse field, you're lucky, and that's where you should sit. But if there aren't any, what do you do? If there are no boundaries, how can you line up on the sideline? Many parents think that sitting behind the goal is a good place because the goal is a defining mark on the field. The problem is that a lot of play goes on behind the goal, much of it crucial to scoring. Just picture your daughter's wrath when the ref has to blow the whistle on the play because you can't get yourself and your beach chair out of the way fast enough.

There are basically two pieces of advice for this problem:

◆ Stand near a natural boundary.

◆ Stay on your feet.

As crazy as this no-boundary field sounds, it actually works. The girls are working toward the goal, so no one is interested in going too far astray.

HOMESTYLE LACROSSE FUN

Lacrosse is a difficult sport to master, so playing games at home are crucial for your child. The following sections describe some skill-building games your kid can play.

Knock Out

Knock Out is a great game. It's played against a wall with at least three players and a wall that won't be damaged by being constantly hit by the lacrosse ball. (Tennis backboards are a good choice.) It's helpful to draw a line about four feet up, so the thrower can't throw the ball so low it's impossible to catch.

Players get in a line. The first player throws the ball at the wall and then runs to the end of the line. The second player gets the rebound before it hits the ground and throws the ball toward the wall again. Now she runs to the end of the line, and so on. If a player misses a rebound, then she's eliminated. The last person left is the winner.

Hot Potato

Every kid has probably played *Hot Potato* at one time or another, but it can also be a great lacrosse game. You should have at least four players for it.

Players stand in a large circle, set a timer, and begin passing the ball around with their sticks. When the timer goes off, the player left holding the ball (or chasing after it, if he missed) gets a *P* for the first letter of *POTATO*. Players are eliminated when they've spelled out *P-O-T-A-T-O*. The game keeps going until only one person is left.

The players determine who has to chase the ball. If it's a bad throw, then the thrower does. If it's a flubbed catch, then the catcher does.

Double Jeopardy

Double Jeopardy is a good game for four players. Players divide into two teams and stand across from each other at a good throwing distance. Each player on one team throws to the player opposite her on the other. There should be two balls, one on each side. On cue, both teams start passing to the other side. The object is to never allow both balls to be on the same side at the same time. The team that forces its opponents to do this gets a point. However, if the team has two balls on its side because someone had to chase a bad throw, play starts over again with no team getting a point. Play goes to 21 points.

LEARNING THE LINGO

As if the rules aren't hard enough, you have to learn the different lacrosse terms, too. The following table will help you on your way.

Lacrosse lingo	
TERM	*EXPLANATION*
basket	The net part of the lacrosse stick.
body-checking	Hitting the opponent with the body (legal only in boys' lacrosse).

TERM	EXPLANATION
center	The midfielder who takes the face-off (boys' lacrosse) or the draw (girls' lacrosse).
checking	Hitting an opponent's stick.
cover point	The middle defense player in girls' lacrosse.
cradling	Carrying the ball in the stick while running.
crease	The circle around the goal where only the goalie is allowed to play.
crosse	The lacrosse stick.
draw	At the beginning of the girls' game, two players hold their sticks up in the air and trap the ball between the backs of the baskets.
face	Another term for *face-off*.
face-off	At the beginning of the boys' game, two players hold their sticks on the ground, trapping the ball between the backs of the baskets.
first home	The frontmost attacker in girls' lacrosse.
free position	The restart of play after a foul has occurred, in which the fouled player gets possession of the ball and everyone is cleared at least five yards away.
goal area	The area in boys' lacrosse where the attack players must remain during the face-off.
goalkeeper	The player protecting the goal and the only player allowed in the crease.
left attack wing	One of the side players in girls' lacrosse.
left defense wing	One of the side players in girls' lacrosse.
point	The defensive player in girls' lacrosse who is closest to the goalkeeper.

continues

TERM	EXPLANATION
poke-checking	Jabbing at a player with the stick (legal only in boys' lacrosse).
right attack wing	One of the side players in girls' lacrosse.
right defense wing	One of the side players in girls' lacrosse.
second home	The second attacker in girls' lacrosse.
third home	The attacker third in line in girls' lacrosse, closest to the midfield.
third man	The defensive player closest to the center in girls' lacrosse.
throw	When the ref in girls' lacrosse restarts the ball by tossing it between two players.
wing area	The portion of the field where the side midfielders must remain until the ref blows the whistle for the face-off.

Almost without exception, athletes who have played lacrosse will tell you it's their favorite sport. Even though the boys' and girls' games differ dramatically, this fondness for the sport cuts across the gender gap. In fact, probably the only people who don't like it are the parents who haven't quite figured it out yet.

THE LEAST YOU NEED TO KNOW

◆ Lacrosse is a fast-paced game that uses sticks topped with baskets to move the ball down the field and into a goal.

◆ There are two versions of the game: one for boys and one for girls.

◆ The boys' games is somewhat physical, so it requires pads and helmets.

◆ The girls' game is a noncontact sport and has no boundaries.

Hitting the Rink for Ice Hockey

In This Chapter

◆ Rink, rules, and equipment

◆ Making the time and money commitment

◆ Learning the lingo

Ice hockey is probably the fastest game in the world. The skaters and the puck fly around a small rink at incredible speeds. The Fox Network even went so far as to develop a glowing puck to help TV viewers follow the game. If your child is going to play the sport well, he must have super reflexes, be a top-notch skater, and be in excellent shape.

Ice hockey, like most other sports, has downsides and upsides. The downsides are the high injury rate and the costs of paying for ice time, buying new skates, and replacing broken sticks. And, to quote one hockey mom, "Then there's the fact that I'm always so cold."

However, the upsides are hard to argue with. Both mom and kid will be treated to an exciting, fast-paced game that's rising in popularity. Both girls and boys can play, and unlike basketball or football, size is not a limiting factor in ice hockey. All that's really needed is a *hockey personality*—being someone who loves to compete, loves speed, and can be aggressive and can handle aggression in return.

This chapter goes into more detail on the time and money involved in playing ice hockey. It also explains the rules, the positions, and those confusing lines all over the ice. It wraps up with some games and terms you might need if your child is going to be a hockey player.

BET YOU DIDN'T KNOW

The origins of ice hockey are disputed. There's one camp that says it evolved from field hockey and another that says it came from cricket. Both agree, however, that it was Canada's long icy winters that led athletes in the frozen north to try to play this sport.

PUT IT ON ICE

The hockey *rink* is an ice surface that's 200 feet by 85 feet with rounded corners. It's enclosed by a four-foot-high wall, called the *boards*. Most of the boards are topped by shatterproof barriers to protect the fans.

The playing surface is crossed horizontally by red and blue lines. There are three red lines. One, a foot wide, divides the ice in half. The other two red lines, each two inches wide, are 10 feet in from the ends of the rink and are called the *goal lines*. In the center of each goal line is the goal. The goal is four feet tall and six feet wide. In front of the goal is a four-by-eight-foot box called the *crease*.

Two blue lines, each a foot wide, divide the rink into thirds. From the goal line to the first blue line is 30 feet; this area is called the *end zone* (or an *attacking zone* or a *defending zone*, depending on the team). From that blue line to the next blue line, another 30 feet, is the *neutral zone*, and then another end zone. (I'll explain all these lines later.)

There are four red *face-off circles*, two on each end, and one blue circle in the center with a one-foot-diameter red spot in the center of that. All in all, with the white ice and red and blue lines, it's quite a patriotic playing surface.

PAD UP

Have you ever wondered why there are so many secondhand skate stores? Ice hockey moms quickly find out the answer when their children outgrow their $100 pair of skates and doubly expensive set of gear after only one season. Unlike other sports, the equipment isn't included as part of the league membership fee. Each player has to provide her own.

From bottom to top, here's a list of the necessary equipment:

- **skates**   They must be specifically hockey skates. No figure skates or racing skates need apply.

- **ankle guards**   They go over the skate.

- **shin guards**

- **garters**   They hold the shin pads up.

- **knee protectors**

- **padded pants**   They offer some protection to the thigh area.

- **supporter and cup**

- **gloves**   They are large, thick, and heavily padded in the fingers and backs of the hand. The front is less padded so that the player can get a good grip on the stick.

- **stick**   To get the right size, rest it on its tip. The end should be about mouth high (chin high if your child is wearing skates). The angle of the head varies and will depend on your child's playing style, but start with a medium angle.

- **elbow pads**

- **shoulder pads**

- **mouthguard**

- **helmet**

- **uniform**   Not just the little $6 T-shirt you get for soccer; it's a heavy numbered shirt, plus shorts and socks.

You get the picture. (And don't even ask about the goalie equipment.) It's going to be a big bill. Obviously, protective equipment is something you don't want to skimp on. You might think you can get away with cheap skates, but those without a good blade or good support in the ankles will end up causing injuries. Fortunately, many secondhand skate shops do exist, and they buy and sell all the used protective equipment, too.

Aside from the expense of this equipment, there's another downside: There's so much of it! There's not a hockey mom around who can't tell you how her kid forgot this or that piece of equipment and how she had to end up buying a replacement at the expensive rink store because the place they were playing was an hour from home.

INSTANT REPLAY

The captain and star of a Bantam League team, a young boy named Marshall, put his team and his mother in a tight spot. When they got to the rink after a 45-minute drive, he realized he'd left his skates at home. That was one thing his mother refused to replace. She thought about driving back, but the round trip would bring her back to the rink right at the end of the game. It didn't make sense. The team was panicked they'd have to play the game without their star, but the skate shop finally came through. Someone had left a pair of skates for sharpening and they just happened to be the right size. Marshall grabbed them, helped his team win the game, and never forgot his skates again.

A SPEEDY OVERVIEW OF A SPEEDY GAME

Ice hockey is played in three 20-minute periods. The object is to score more goals than the opposing team.

The play begins with a *face-off*. The *center* (the middle player on the front line) on each team meets in the center circle. The referee drops the *puck*, a hard rubber disk, on the spot on the center of the ice. After that, the puck must be kept in motion at all times. Each center tries to get control. The face-off also occurs at the beginning of each period, after a goal, and after the whistle has blown for a foul.

There are six players on an ice hockey team: the *goalkeeper*, *right defense*, *left defense*, *center*, *right wing*, and *left wing* (the wings are often referred to as the *forwards*). The centers try to get the puck out to their wings and the three of them mount an attack on the opponent's goal.

They may pass the puck or move it up the rink themselves. They use their sticks to maneuver the puck, but they may also kick it with the blades of their skates (although they may not score that way). When they get in front of the goal, they shoot the puck at it. If it crosses the goal line, it's a goal, worth one point.

The defense, meanwhile, tries to stop the other team from making a goal. They try to physically block the skaters with their bodies, *checking* them with their hips or shoulders whenever possible. Body-checking is legal only from the front and side, not from the back.

The defensive players also try to get control of the puck with their sticks so that they can send it up to the offensive players. They can try to hit the other player's stick, go for the puck, or intercept a pass or shot. Players may block a puck with their hands, but they must drop it right down in front of them. Throwing or carrying the puck is not allowed.

Stick-checking is also a large part of defense. There are three types of stick-checking:

◆ **poke-checking**   Jabbing the blade of the stick at the puck.

◆ **hook-checking**   Reaching in from behind with the stick.

◆ **sweep-checking**   Laying the stick on the ice and sliding it toward the puck.

Although the three forwards are primarily offense and the two defensive players (the right and left defense positions) are primarily defense, all five work together for both offense and defense. In other words, when the team has the puck, the defense moves up, too. Sometimes they even take the puck all the way up to shoot it in the goal, and a wing must drop back to cover. When an offensive player loses the puck, he doesn't just turn around and watch the game proceed without him. He immediately tries to get it back, using defensive maneuvers and hassling the guy who stole it from him. This flexibility allows the whole team to get into position to defend the goal.

Subbing

Hockey doesn't allow any timeouts (unless, of course, there's an injury), so a coach must take her players out of the game to talk to them. Fortunately, this is easy to do. *Subbing* is totally free. Players can skate on and off the ice at any time, as many times as they like, without notifying the ref. Aside from getting to chat with the coach, subbing is also done to give players a break from this grueling sport. (In fact, that's really the prime reason for subbing.)

Players usually go in and out as a *line*: the three offensive players go off at once while three new ones come on, and the defensive players go off and on the same way. The lines have practiced together and are familiar with how each other moves, so there's a real advantage to this method of substituting.

A line stays in for about two minutes before sitting out for a breather. This length of play is about all a coach can expect if she wants her players performing at peak level.

Line Up

The game seems pretty easy, you think. So what, pray tell, are all the lines for? The goal line is easy; it marks where the goal should be. Players are allowed to skate over the goal line behind the goal.

However, the other lines are a little more complicated. The two blue lines dividing the rink into thirds serve two purposes. No attacking player can cross the blue line that marks the attacking zone ahead of the puck. Doing so is called *offsides*. Easy, right? However, if the puck is hit out of the zone, recovered, and hit back into it before an attacking player can get out of the zone, then the attacking player isn't called offsides if she doesn't touch the puck.

The blue lines also ensure that the puck is brought up the ice in a controlled manner, rather than slapped up and down the length of the rink. Passes must go from a player in the defensive zone to a player in the neutral zone to a player in the attacking zone. In other words, a pass may not cross two blue lines.

If either of these violations occur, there's a face-off in the offending team's end zone.

Icing is a tricky rule in hockey because there seem to be so many exceptions to it. This rule is where the center red line comes into play. A player may not send the puck across the opponent's goal line if that player is behind the red line. This move is called icing; if it occurs, the puck is brought back to the offending team's end for a face-off. It seems so simple, doesn't it?

However, it isn't icing if one of the following happens:

◆ The puck goes into the goal.

◆ The goalie is the one who retrieves the puck.

◆ The team who hit the puck in the first place is the first one to touch the puck.

◆ If the team who commits icing is short one or more players.

You've got to wonder why they even bother.

The Penalty Box

When a *penalty* occurs, the ref waits until the offending team has the puck. He then sends the player who committed the penalty to the penalty box for a few minutes; the length of the penalty depends on the infraction. That team must play short a player until the penalty time is up. Play then resumes with a face-off in one of the red circles, the end depending on which team committed the penalty.

Here are some of the most common penalties you will see:

◆ **holding**   Actually grabbing onto a player.

◆ **high sticks**   Lifting the stick to around the player's head level.

◆ **slashing**   Hitting a player with the stick.

◆ **cross-checking**   Checking a player illegally.

◆ **tripping**

◆ **fighting**

When one or two players are in the penalty box, the other team is said to have a *power play*. They send all five of their players into the attacking zone, hoping to overpower the short-handed team. Many times, a goal is scored in this situation. The team that's short concentrates mainly on protecting the goal. They put their best *penalty killers* out, the players who have practiced this situation. It's not a time that a team wants to be on the offensive. One of the best things a penalty killer can do is send the puck all the way down the ice. Remember, it's not icing if you're short-handed.

A Final Word About the Goalkeeper

In hockey, the goalie doesn't come in and out like the rest of the team, although she certainly can. She wears a different set of pads and has long flat skates and a different stick. She's the only player who is allowed to catch the puck, which she does in something that looks like a baseball glove.

The crease around the goal is the goalkeeper's alone. No other player is allowed in there. However, the goalie is allowed out of the crease, just not beyond the red line in the center. The goalie needs to have this buffer zone because the puck moves so fast that she'd be lost if the players could skate right in. As it is, being the goalie (also called the *netminder*) in ice hockey is one of the hardest jobs an athlete can have.

Sometimes, in the final moments of the game, a team will pull its goalie from the goal and put in a sixth player, hoping to over-power the other team in front of the goal.

THE COMMITMENT

You can see now why hockey holds such appeal. When your child asks to try it, it's hard to say no. Look out! There's a whole lot more involved. I'm not saying you shouldn't embrace this sport, but I do think all parents should be aware of what's to come.

If the sport remains a casual, fun hobby, you're in good shape. However, if your child wants to play in high school and college, things are going to get much more difficult.

Have an Ice Time

To play ice hockey properly, you need ice, obviously. (Many players also play street hockey on in-line skates during the warm weather, but it just isn't the same.) The problem is that for nearly everyone but those Minnesotans in their frozen land of 10,000 lakes, ice is scarce. If your child is going to play seriously, he's going to want to be on the ice more than his once-a-week league.

Unfortunately, the leagues are the lowest of the low when it comes to rink time. College teams, high school teams, adult leagues, and figure skating commitments all rank over the kids. You're going to find yourself driving to rinks at 6:00 a.m. before school or at 9:00 p.m., which is a little late for a 10-year-old. On top of it all, you're paying through the nose for this thoroughly inconvenient ice time.

School Play

And the difficulties just increase. Now your son is 13...he's been playing ice hockey for five years, he's one of the top scorers on his club's team, and he loves the sport. Unfortunately, the local high school doesn't have an ice hockey team. The private school two towns over does, but once again, your commitment level will have to escalate. Do you spend the money and travel time, or does your son's involvement stop there?

A Year-Round Proposition

Many mothers have found out that ice hockey becomes a year-round proposition. Nearly all the leagues play nine months out of the year. It's not just a once-a-week deal, either. Practices are usually held two or three times a week, with a game on the weekend.

INJURIES

The good news is that the ice hockey you see the pros playing, with violent checking escalating into fights, isn't exactly the ice hockey your child will be playing. Most school organizations and ice hockey leagues prohibit that kind of behavior on the ice (one wonders why the pros can't!).

However, the truth is (and here's the bad news) that hockey is still an injury-prone sport. Basically, the padding decreases and the violence escalates as the players move up a level. The checking, the high-speed skating, the swinging sticks, and the flying puck make it slightly more dangerous than, say, tennis.

Most people think that hockey injuries stem mainly from the fights and the checking, but a puck flying at 100 mph can do some damage, too. One hockey player I know got a puck in the throat, severing his esophagus. He was on life support and in intensive care for a week. His esophagus was sewn together with no lasting damage, although his voice became slightly lower. If the puck had hit his larynx, only a half inch away, he would have been left with no voice.

The worst injuries generally come from kids fooling around without their protective gear on. Making sure kids wear their padding is your primary responsibility as a hockey mom.

INSTANT REPLAY

One cloudy afternoon during a pick-up game on a lake, a 10-year-old boy, totally unprotected, skated in front of a slapshot at the wrong moment. The puck flew into his knee, shattering the kneecap. Pete's ice hockey career was over in an instant, and many other sports were off-limits for life too.

ICE IDEAS

Occasionally a hockey player might find herself on a frozen pond, looking for a game to play. Some fun ones are described in the following sections.

Slapshot

Slapshot couldn't be simpler, yet kids love to play it. One player is the goalie, and the other player is the shooter. The shooter has 10 chances to fire a slapshot past the goalie. Then the players switch positions, with the other player now having 10 shots. The first player to get to 21 goals is the winner, although both players must have an equal number of turns. If they both go over 21, then the player with the most goals wins.

It's a good idea to have a line at least a couple of yards away from the goal to limit how close the shooter can get.

Duck

In *Duck*, players form a large circle, with fairly large gaps between each player; you should have quite a few players for this game. Everyone should have a stick and a puck. One player is the duck, and he skates around the circle, keeping the puck close to him at all times. At some point, he skates between two people into the center of the circle. Those two people must take off in opposite directions with their pucks and get all the way around the circle and back into their spots. The faster one gets to be the new duck, and the old duck moves out of the center into his spot.

LEARNING THE LINGO

If your teeth aren't chattering too much as you're standing around the rink, you might want to chat with the other parents. The following table lists some ice hockey terms you can use.

Ice hockey lingo	
TERM	*EXPLANATION*
attacking zone	The area between the opponent's blue line and goal line.
boards	The four-foot-high wall around the rink.
body-checking	Throwing a hip or shoulder into another skater.
clear	Sending the puck away from the goal.
crease	The area around the goal where only the goalie is allowed to be.
defending zone	The area between a player's goal line and the first blue line.
face-off	The way the puck is put back in play; the referee drops the puck between two opposing players who are standing in a face-off circle.

continues

TERM	EXPLANATION
hat trick	One player scoring three goals in one game.
icing	Shooting the puck from behind the center line over the opponent's goal line.
offsides	When an attacking player is ahead of the puck in the attacking zone.
penalty box	Where a player must sit if he's committed a foul.
penalty killer	Playing when you're down one player.
power play	Playing when you're up one player.
stick checking	Using the stick to try to get the puck away from an opposing player.

Ice hockey is a fast-paced, exciting sport. If your kids are playing it, they'll be in incredible shape and will learn skills that serve them well in other sports. As far as you're concerned, if you can follow the puck around the rink, you've won half the battle.

THE LEAST YOU NEED TO KNOW

◆ Ice hockey is played between two teams of six players on an ice rink.

◆ Players on ice skates pass the puck by using sticks in an effort to get the puck into the goal.

◆ Lines on the rink create restrictions on how far the puck can move.

◆ The game requires lots of time and money.

Football Fun

Football is a purely American game, embodying the country's best and worst traits. A larger-than-life sport, costing—yet also producing—gobs of money, it's a rough-and-tumble game that combines finesse and brute force.

The Super Bowl, football's ultimate contest, is the most watched (and most gambled on) event in television. At high schools and colleges, football games are big social events, with tailgate and homecoming parties centered on them. Is it any wonder that your son is dying to be part of this spectacle?

Yet part of you can't get past the bone-crushing, back-cracking, neck-snapping, knee-destroying hits and tackles that seem to be a huge part of the game.

Well, here's the good news. Football protective equipment has improved dramatically over the past few decades and will continue to, and injury rates go down every year. For the youngest kids, the number of football injuries isn't any higher than the number of injuries caused by any other sport. (By high school, however, football injury rates are high.)

So get your sons onto the gridiron, and get your nose into this chapter. It tells you all you need to know about the field and its markings, the positions and their names, and the rules and the scoring. It winds up with some backyard fun and football lingo.

BET YOU DIDN'T KNOW

Football historians will tell you that the first official "football" game was played between Princeton University and Rutgers University on November 6, 1869, but today's football fan would hardly recognize the sport played at that game. There were 25 men on each team, and the game was much closer to soccer than football. Harvard University, which had developed a soccer-style game in which players could pick up the ball and run with it, and McGill University in Canada, which played rugby, created a combination of the two games that eventually became American football.

BETWEEN THE UPRIGHTS

Football is played on a field 360 feet long and 160 feet wide, shown in the following figure. At each *end line* are *goalposts*, which are two upright posts, 24 feet apart, and a *crossbar*, 10 feet off the ground. The field is divided in half by the *50-yard line*. Moving away from the 50-yard line in five-yard intervals are more horizontal lines crossing the field. In 10-yard intervals, numbers on the field count down the lines to zero, that is, the 40-yard line, the 30-yard line, and so on. The zero-yard line is called the *goal line*.

In the center of the field, from goal line to goal line, are hash-marks indicating the one-yard intervals. Two columns of them line up with the two uprights of the goalposts. The last 10 yards between the goal line and the end line is called the *end zone*.

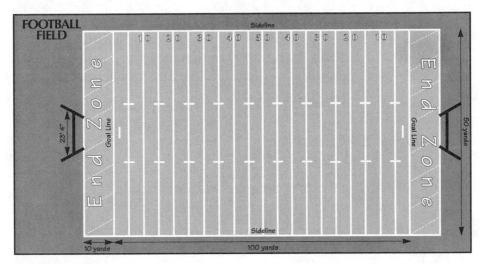

The football field.

PROTECTING YOUR YOUNG

Football is a rough sport, but over the years more and more pads and protective gear have been added to keep injuries to a minimum. That's the good news. The bad news is that all this equipment makes football a very expensive sport, and it still doesn't make it risk free.

A football player wears a helmet with a face mask and a chin guard and protective pads on nearly every part of the body. He wears cleats and a mouthguard, too.

Football is played with an oblong ball that comes to a point on each end. It's generally made of pigskin, and it has laces along one side.

GETTING IN POSITION

There are 11 players on a team. In professional football, college ball, and some large high schools, there are actually many more than 11 players who play each game, even though there are still only 11 out on the field at any one time. The game has gotten so sophisticated that there are 11 players just for offense, 11 for defense, and a few others who play only on the *special teams* (the kick return team, the field goal team, the punt team, and so on); they are mainly the kickers.

So even though your kids won't be using this huge arsenal of players, I'll explain the positions as though they were. That way, even if your son never goes out of the game, you'll know that on offense he was a wide receiver, on defense he was a cornerback, on a punt return he was a blocker, and so forth.

The Scoring Machine

Let's begin with the 11 offensive positions. The rules dictate that the offense must have at least seven players within one foot of the *line of scrimmage*, which is the imaginary line running the width of the field where the ball is placed at the start of each play. (The location of the line of scrimmage changes as the ball progresses down the field.)

The seven players generally include the *wide receiver*, the *tight end*, two *tackles*, two *guards*, and a *center*. Behind the center is the *quarterback* and somewhere in back of him are a *halfback* and a *fullback*. The *halfback* and *fullback* are also called *running backs*. The eleventh player is another wide receiver, another tight end, or another running back.

Here's a description of each position's duties:

- **quarterback**   He runs the show. He calls the plays, and then takes the ball from the center to pass it, run with it, or hand it off to another runner.

- **center**   He snaps the ball at the start of each play. Once the ball is snapped, he joins the other lineman guarding the quarterback or blocking for the runner.

- **guard** and **tackle**   They line up on the line of scrimmage and have two different jobs, depending on what play the offense is running. If it's a passing play, they try to block the defense from getting through to the quarterback. If it's a running play, they try to push the defensive players aside so the runner can get through.

- **tight end**   This player either blocks the defense or goes out for a pass, depending on the play.

- **wide receiver**   This player is the primary passing target and blocks during running plays.

- **halfback** and **fullback**   The players who get the hand-off from the quarterback and then try to run with the ball. The halfback is usually faster and smaller and the fullback is usually bigger and more powerful.

BET YOU DIDN'T KNOW

In the early days of football, there weren't many rules restricting what could be done to keep a player from getting the quarterback. Linemen didn't get low to the ground, but instead stood up and went at each other on the snap. They essentially had to learn how to box and wrestle, both as aggressors and defenders. By the end of the game, players were often bloodied, and there were several deaths on the field over the years. After one especially bloody game was publicized, President Theodore Roosevelt threatened to make a law abolishing the sport unless some rules were changed. Therefore, the forward pass was added, the punching was eliminated, and the game was cleaned up a bit.

The Defense Never Rests

The defense doesn't have the same line of scrimmage restrictions that the offense has, although they generally have at least three or four players right on the line, too. The defensive positions usually include two *tackles*, two *ends*, three *linebackers*, two *cornerbacks*, and two *safeties*. The cornerbacks and safeties are sometimes lumped together under the title of *defensive backs*.

Here's what the defensive players do:

- **tackles** and **ends**   Usually the heaviest men on the team. They watch to see whether the next play will be a running play or a passing play. If it's a running play, they stay where they are and try to stop the runner. If it's a passing play, they try to get through the offensive line to *sack* (tackle) the quarterback before the pass.

- **linebacker**   The middle defense guys, about five yards off the line of scrimmage. They go after the quarterback on a passing play, cover running backs on a passing play, or try to tackle the runner on a running play.

♦ **cornerback**   These players cover the wide receivers and try to stop them from getting the pass. They also try to tackle the runner on running plays.

♦ **safety**   These players are the last line of defense. They go after the long ball pass or runners who have gotten by the other defensive players.

All defensive players are on the lookout for loose balls, called *fumbles*. If a ball pops out of an offensive player's hands, it's up for grabs, so whoever dives on it first gets possession. The defense can also get control of the ball by intercepting a pass.

The following figure shows what the positions look like when you put them all together.

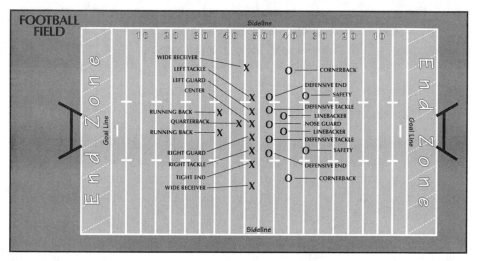

The offensive and defensive positions.

Kickers

What about the kickers, you ask? This is, after all, a game called *foot*ball. When and where do the only players who actually use their feet come into the game? These players are brought on during the kicking plays. There are two types of kickers, and most teams have a different kicker for each type of kick (although with young kids, teams may have the same kicker do both). One type of kicker is the *place kicker*, who kicks the ball off the ground. The other is the *punter*, who drop-kicks the ball out of his hand. The rules define which kick is allowed at which time.

RULES TO PLAY BY

The game is made up of four *quarters*. The time of each quarter varies, depending on the level of play (pros use 15-minute quarters). The object is to move the ball down the field until, in one of a variety of ways, the team gets the ball over the goal line, thus scoring points. The team with the most points at the end of the game is the winner.

The Kick-off

Play begins with a *kick-off*. The ball is placed on a tee on the kicking team's 35-yard line. During the kick-off, a team generally wants the ball to go as far down field as possible, but it must go at least 10 yards. The other team tries to catch the kick and run it back. The play stops when the player with the ball is tackled. Kick-offs are also used at the start of the half (but not the start of the second or fourth quarters) and after a score.

As a last-ditch effort at the end of the game, a team who's losing might try an *onside kick*. They kick the ball the minimum 10 yards and try to pounce on it themselves. If they get it before the other team, then the ball is theirs again.

Running the Offense

Once the team has received the kick-off, it's time to run the offense. Each team has several plays that it runs; these plays have code numbers. The team gets in a *huddle*, and the quarterback announces the play that's going to be run, using the code numbers. Then the players all line up in their positions.

The center has his hand on the ball. When all the players are lined up, the quarterback announces the play (in the code numbers) and then says "hut 1, hut 2, hut 3." One of those "huts" is the signal, determined in the huddle, for the center to hike the ball back to the quarterback. All but one of the offensive players must remain stationary until this snap.

The quarterback then hands the ball off to a running back for a running play, passes the ball to a receiver, or runs with it himself. Running plays are pretty straightforward. The runner just tries to get the ball as far up the field as he can before he's tackled or pushed out of bounds. Whatever yard line he is tackled on (or pushed out on) is where the next play begins.

A passing play is alittle more complicated. The quarterback is allowed to throw to the wide receivers, the running backs, and the tight ends. The pass must be thrown from behind the line of scrimmage. The quarterback usually drops way back to get away from the defense while he waits for the receivers to get down field and into position. If the receiver catches the pass before it hits the ground, it's called a *completion*, and he tries to run it for even more yardage. If he misses, then the ball is moved back to wherever it was at the start of the play. If the defense catches it, it's called an *interception*.

The quarterback isn't the only player who can make a forward pass. As long as the pass comes from behind the line of scrimmage, anyone back there can do it. In fact, one sneaky play has the quarterback handing the ball off the to the halfback as though he were starting a running play. The defenders move forward to tackle him, and the receivers are all left free behind. The halfback makes a short pass to a receiver, and he's off and running.

Passes can also be made in front of the line of scrimmage, but they must be backward passes. Even though the pass is going in the wrong direction, it can help get the ball away from the defenders.

INSTANT REPLAY

 On one Pop Warner team, there was a little guy named Walter, who could be knocked to the ground by a defender's little pinky. But Walter was really fast. The coach figured that if he could somehow get the ball to Walter and away from the defenders, the team could take advantage of Walter's speed.

The coach decided to use a play called the *double reverse*. Walter lined up way out to the side on the line of scrimmage. The quarterback handed the ball to the halfback, who started running to the sideline where Walter was waiting. The halfback then handed the ball back to Walter, who ran in the other direction. The defensive players saw what happened, but their momentum was still carrying them toward the sideline. In the time it took for them to shift gears, Walter had sprinted past them and was on his way down the field for a touchdown.

The play worked great game after game, and Walter quickly became the team's leading scorer. However, the few times the play failed and the defense crushed tiny Walter were enough for Walter's mother. That spectacular season was Walter's only one.

Getting a First Down

The offense has four tries, called *downs*, to move the ball 10 yards down the field. If it makes the 10 yards in four or fewer plays, then it gets four more tries. This procedure is called getting a *first down*. If the offense can't get the ball 10 yards in four tries, then it's the other team's ball.

Choosing to Punt

If the team hasn't gotten 10 yards after the third down, it may choose to *punt*. In this case, a player kicks the ball as far and as high as he can. The rest of the team races down the field, hoping to tackle the player who catches the punt. Teams choose to punt on the fourth down to get their opponents as far away from their goal line as possible. Otherwise, if they fail to get a first down, the opponents get the ball in the same place.

The punt is different from the kick-off in that the punting team may not regain possession of the ball (unless the punt receiver fumbles). The players may, however, go after the ball themselves because the place they touch it becomes the line of scrimmage. They might do this to keep the other team from picking up the ball and running with it and also to keep the ball from going into the end zone. If the punt does go into the end zone, then it's brought out to the 20-yard line, which becomes the line of scrimmage.

A punt receiver may signal a *fair catch* by raising an arm up in the air. This means that if he catches it, he won't run with it. The ball will be played from that point. He does this to protect himself if the defense is practically on top of him; he knows he will get creamed and probably not get any more yardage after he catches it, anyway. He might also want to signal a fair catch and then not catch the ball, hoping to slow down the defense so they can't stop the ball from rolling into the end zone.

Touchdown!

If a team is successful and runs the ball or catches a pass across the goal line, then it has scored a *touchdown*, worth six points. After each touchdown, a team is then allowed a *conversion*. The ball is placed on the two-yard line. For one point, the team can kick the ball through the goalposts. Say the team snaps the ball seven yards back to the holder, who sets the ball up for the place kicker. If the team feels it needs two points, it can run another play, either running or passing, and see if it gets the ball over the goal line again. Most teams go for the one-point conversion because it's much easier to make. However, sometimes at the end of the game, the two-point conversion can mean the difference between a win and a tie or a tie and a loss, so teams often try it.

Teams can score points in two other ways: *field goals* and *safeties*. When a team has been unsuccessful in getting a first down, but it has moved the ball a considerable way down the field, it may opt for a field goal, rather than a punt or a play, on the fourth down. A field goal is a place kick. If it goes between the uprights, the team scores three points and kicks off to the other team. If the kick misses, the other team gets the ball at the original line of scrimmage.

A safety, which is a rare occurrence, is worth two points. It happens when the offense has the ball deep in its defensive end and is somehow pushed back and tackled in the other team's end zone.

A FLAG ON THE PLAY

When a player commits a penalty, one or more of the refs throw a flag on the field to signal a penalty on the play. A penalty can be either declined or accepted at the end of the play by the non-offending team. If it's declined, then play goes on as before. (I'll tell you why a team might decline a penalty later in the chapter.) If it's accepted, then the down is replayed, and the ball is moved forward (if the penalty was against the defense) or backward (if the penalty was against the offense).

There are about 60 different penalties, but you'll probably see only a handful of them in Pop Warner ball. Here are the most common penalties:

- **defensive holding** When a defensive player grabs onto an offensive player who is eligible for a pass. This penalty is a five-yard gain for the offense, plus an automatic first down.

- **offensive holding** When any offensive player grabs onto any other player. Ten yards.

- **clipping** When an offensive player blocks somebody whose back is toward him. Fifteen yards.

- **offsides** When any part of a player (on offense or defense) crosses the line of scrimmage before the ball is snapped. Five yards.

- **illegal procedure** This is a catch-all term that includes penalties such as more than one back moving before the snap or a lineman moving before the snap. Five yards.

- ◆ **pass interference**   When the defense interferes with some- one trying to catch the ball. Defensive players may go for the ball themselves, but they can't push someone else out of the way. The offense gets the ball at the point of the foul. In other words, if the ball was thrown 50 yards and the defensive play- er pushed the guy just before the catch, the offense gets to move 50 yards. If the interference was on a touchdown pass, then the ball goes on the one-yard line.

- ◆ **face mask**   When a defensive player grabs the face mask of the guy with the ball as he's trying to tackle him. Five yards if it's unintentional, or 15 if it's intentional. This call is obviously up to the ref's judgment.

- ◆ **grounding**   The quarterback throws the ball to nobody just to avoid a sack. Ten yards and the loss of the down.

- ◆ **personal foul**   For unnecessary roughness, tripping, or unsportsmanlike conduct. Fifteen yards.

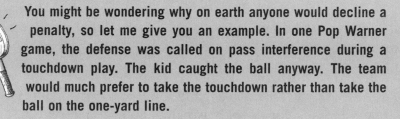

TAKING A CLOSER LOOK

You might be wondering why on earth anyone would decline a penalty, so let me give you an example. In one Pop Warner game, the defense was called on pass interference during a touchdown play. The kid caught the ball anyway. The team would much prefer to take the touchdown rather than take the ball on the one-yard line.

PLAYING WITH THE PIGSKIN

Ever play a big game of pick-up football in the backyard or in the park? It's a rip-roaring, ripped-clothing kind of time. But what happens on the average Sunday afternoon? You're in the mood to play, but the teams just aren't big enough. The following sections describe some other options.

Quarterback Golf

Quarterback Golf is a great game for two players who both want to be the quarterback. The players set up "holes" wherever they're playing. These "holes" are really just targets, such as cans or trees. The targets should be progressively farther away from the throwing area.

One player snaps the ball, and the other drops back and throws at the first target. Once both players have hit the first target, they start throwing at the second one, and so on. Players keep track of the number of throws it takes to reach the targets; the player with the fewest throws is the winner.

Ultimate Football

If you have six or more players, *Ultimate Football* is a fun game to play. It's basically Ultimate Frisbee using a football. There are two end lines. One team starts on its end of the field and kicks off to the other team. One player on this team receives the ball and then tries to move it down the field by passing it to a teammate. Players may not run with the ball. Passes can go in any direction, forward or backward. If the ball lands on the ground, it's up for grabs. The defending team tries to intercept the passes or pick up loose balls. Each time a team throws a completed pass over the endline, it scores a point. The first team to score 10 points is the winner.

Animal Ball

Little kids like this somewhat brutal game. *Animal Ball* is for three or four players. One player, the quarterback, calls out a play, such as "fifteen yards out, cut left," and then throws the ball. The receivers battle each other for the ball. Whoever catches the ball gets to be the next quarterback. If no one catches the ball, the same quarterback goes again.

LEARNING THE LINGO

There's quite a bit of time between each play, so you can always ask your neighbor in the bleachers to explain a term. However, if you want to learn some football terms on your own, the following table lists the most common.

Football lingo	
TERM	EXPLANATION
50-yard line	The line dividing the field in half.
center	The lineman who snaps the ball.
completion	A pass that makes it from the quarterback to the receiver without hitting the ground.
conversion	The extra point or points that can be earned after a touchdown.
cornerback	A defensive back who usually tries to cover the receivers.
defensive back	The defensive players who are the farthest back from the line of scrimmage.
down	A try or play. Teams are allowed four of them.
end	A defensive lineman.
end line	The ends of the field, 10 yards beyond each goal line.
end zone	The area between the goal line and the end line where a touchdown is scored.
fair catch	When a player signals he won't run a kick back, so he can avoid being tackled.
field goal	When the ball is kicked through the goalposts on the fourth down. It's worth three points.
fullback	A player who runs with the ball.
fumble	When a player drops the ball.
goal line	The zero-yard lines on each end of the field.

TERM	EXPLANATION
goalposts	The two upright posts on the end line through which the ball must pass during a conversion or a field goal.
guard	An offensive lineman.
halfback	An offensive player who runs the ball.
huddle	When the team meets to plan a play.
interception	When the defense catches a pass.
kick-off	The start of play at the beginning of a half or after a score.
line of scrimmage	The place where the ball is put at the start of the play. Neither team may cross this line until the ball is snapped.
linebacker	The middle line of defense.
onside kick	A kick on the kick-off that goes only slightly more than 10 yards.
place kicker	The player who kicks the ball for a field goal, kick-off, or conversion.
punter	The player who kicks the ball on the fourth down.
running back	A player who runs with the ball.
sack	When the quarterback is tackled behind the line of scrimmage.
safety (position)	The last line of defense.
safety (score)	When a team is tackled in its opponent's end zone. Worth two points to the defensive team.
special teams	The group of people who take the field during a kick.

continues

Football lingo *continued*	
TERM	*EXPLANATION*
snap	When the center hands the ball to the quarterback.
tackle	An offensive or defensive line player.
tight end	An offensive player who can run, pass, or block.
touchdown	Crossing the goal line with the ball. Worth six points.
wide receiver	An offensive player who is the primary target for a pass.

Football is such a part of American life that even if your son decides the sport isn't for him, you might want to bone up on the rules for your own sake. At the next Superbowl party you're invited to, at least you'll be able to talk about the unusual offensive formation instead of the unusual spice your hosts put in the chili.

THE LEAST YOU NEED TO KNOW

◆ Football is a game between two teams of 11 players each; it's played on a football field.

◆ The object is to move the ball over the goal line, by running or passing, without being tackled.

◆ Points can also be scored by kicking the ball through the goalposts.

◆ Football is a rougher sport than most others, making the protective gear a crucial part of the game.

10

Volleyball: Not Just for Picnics Anymore

It's hard to imagine there's someone out there who hasn't encountered volleyball at one time or another. At picnics, there always seems to be a net strung up somewhere with people recruiting fellow picnickers to join in a game. Rules are fuzzy, skills are minimal, but fun is had by all.

If your son or daughter finds a position on the high school team, however, it will be a whole new ball game. (Almost. They'll probably still have fun.)

This chapter introduces you to the rules, the specialized positions each player fills, and the strategy most teams use to get a point. Some pick-up games are included, as are some terms to help you communicate with your new volleyball player.

HOLDING COURT

In the United States, the volleyball court is 60 feet by 30 feet. (See Figure 10.1.) A court is divided in half lengthwise by the *center line*, creating two squares. The net is placed over the center line, eight feet high for boys and seven feet, four and a half inches high for girls.

The net extends over the sidelines, so the poles are outside the court. Vertical tape runs up the net to mark the edge of the court. Two antennae extend above the net to help the referees make their calls.

At each endline, there's an approximately 10-foot area marked off for the serve, called the *serving box*. This area limits the players' side-to-side movement, but they can move backward as far as they want.

Ten feet back from the center line on each side is a line that marks off the *attack area*. Only players who are standing in front of the attack line at the serve are allowed to hit it over the net from the attack area later.

The equipment is pretty simple: a net and a ball. Many players like to have knee pads and elbow pads as well because there's quite a bit of diving on the floor.

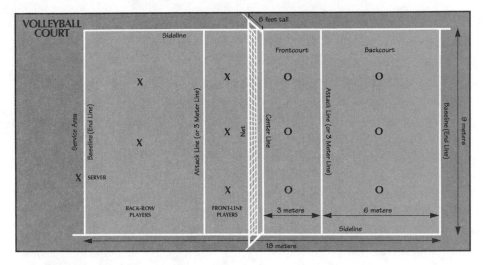

The volleyball court.

LEARNING THE RULES

Each team has six players, three up front and three in the back. (Compare that to the picnic games with anywhere from two to twenty people on a side.)

The object of the game is to score 15 points, winning by two, before the other team does. Only the serving team can score a point. If the receiving team wins the rally, it doesn't get a point, but it does earn the chance to serve. This procedure is called *siding out*.

Play begins with a serve from the serving box. The server must strike the ball with one hand, and the ball must completely clear the net and land within the bounds of the court to be a good serve. A server gets only one chance at a serve.

The receiving team must return the ball in three or fewer touches. The same person may not hit the ball two times in a row (which makes volleyball an excellent game for learning sharing skills). The ball goes back and forth over the net until it either hits the ground, goes out of bounds, or doesn't make it over in a maximum of three touches, which means one of the sides has won the rally. If the serving team has won, it scores a point. If the receiving team has won, it gets the serve (siding out).

No player is ever allowed to touch the net, but the ball may bounce off the net and continue to be played (except on the serve).

Good Things Come in Threes

The three hits a team is allowed aren't just three random pokes at the ball. They each have a purpose.

The first is the *forearm pass* (if coming after a serve) or a *dig* (if coming after an attack). This hit is usually done with the flat area on the fleshy side of the forearms, and it keeps the ball from landing on the floor. The player does her best to direct this hit to the *setter* (the player responsible for the next hit). If the forearm pass comes after an attack rather than a serve, getting the hit to the setter is sometimes harder to do. In that case, its main purpose is to take the sting out of the attack and get the ball high up in the air where it can be more easily manipulated. The player still tries to get it to the setter, however.

The second of the three hits is called the *set*. The ball is placed (or set) in a position that would be advantageous for an attack. It's a gentle, two-handed, mostly fingertip touch.

The third hit is called the *spike*. It's a mean, aggressive, bullet of a hit, usually one-handed and aimed down at the opponent's floor. It's the hit that crosses the net and goes for the kill.

In the Rotation

When the six players are in place at the start of the serve, they take positions referred to as right back, center back, left back, right forward, center forward, and left forward. After each side out, players *rotate* to the next position.

After the serve has been hit, players may move to any spot on the court, but the ones who began in the attack area are still the only ones who can hit the ball over the net from that area. Both front and back row players can hit it over from the back, although it's less desirable to do so because the ball can't be spiked toward the floor.

Players move to take advantage of their different skills. If someone is an excellent forearm passer, for instance, she should move to the back row immediately in preparation for a dig. Keeping her up front would be a waste. Knowing which players will take which positions also cuts down on the confusion over who's going to go after the ball. For instance, a team usually has only one setter. In that case, every single person on the team knows who is going to hit the ball for that second touch.

INSTANT REPLAY

High school volleyball is one of the worst tortures known to girls in a coed gym class; basically, it's 45 minutes of watching the boys play. Because the roles aren't assigned, the boys often seem to think it's their duty to gallantly go after every ball, regardless of who is closest. To top it off, their height gives them an advantage even if the girls stand their ground. Every girl I've ever talked to about this agrees. One even told me of a boy who, in his efforts to be the star, actually pushed her off the court. His own teammate!

Rock Around the Block

Blocking is a defensive tactic. Essentially, one, two, or even three players jump up in front of the other team's attack to try to stop the ball. They may not touch the net (remember, no one is ever allowed to touch the net), but they may reach over it (if they can) after the attack has been made. If they do manage to block it successfully, then the ball bounces back to the other side. If the blockers touch the ball but don't get it back to the other side, the touch does not count as one of the three hits.

LEARNING THE LINEUP

Even though there are six positions on the court, there are really only four roles: the *setter,* the *swing hitters,* the *blockers,* and the *opposite.*

The setter is the gentle one, deftly touching the ball with her fingertips to place it in the perfect area for the attack. If you're more familiar with football, think of the setter as the one who holds the ball for the field goal kicker. The setter is the one who receives the ball and places it in the proper position. The setter is a giver—she never gets the satisfaction of the kill.

The Blockers

The blockers tend to be the biggest players because it helps if they can reach above the net. They are also aggressive and like to block. If a blocker can intimidate a hitter, it works almost as well as blocking the actual hit. Usually, a team has two blockers, and they stand opposite one another on the court. On offense, they are also hitters for the attack.

The Swing Hitters

The swing hitters, despite their name, are the ones who receive or *dig* the attack and try to convert it into a controlled pass to the setter. Instead of size, speed is usually the key to a good swing hitter. Again, two players, standing opposite one another, fill this role, and they are also hitters when they're on attack.

The Opposite

The last role is the opposite. This position is the one opposite the setter and can be filled, oddly enough, by either the team's best hitter or worst hitter. Some teams want their worst hitter there because she'll always be with two other hitters when she's in the front row. Others want their best hitter there, because when the setter is in the front row, there are only two other hitters up there. Suddenly, the option of a good back row hitter is appealing. If your child is an opposite, read her the last two sentences and leave it at that.

THE GAME PLAN

When the serve is hit, the action begins. Everyone jumps into position to fulfill their predefined roles. The setter always goes to the same spot, predictably called the *setter spot*, which is near the net, off to one side. Even when she's in the back row, she moves up to this position. The blocker in the front row moves to the middle, and the rest of the team prepares to dig. If all goes according to plan, the swing hitter gets the ball and sends it neatly to the setter spot.

The setter barely has to shift position. She chooses which hitter is going to get the ball and sets it up perfectly. Teams have their own codes to let everyone know where the ball is going.

Next, the attacker comes in for the kill. Generally, a hard, well-placed hit is most effective, but sometimes the fake-out soft tip can work just as well, especially when it can be placed just to the side of the wall of blockers.

Some attackers like to use the blockers to their advantage. There are two hits that do this: the *high flat* and the *wipe-off*. The high flat is a hit aimed for the back wall, not the floor. The spiker tries to hit a low, hard, flat shot that will tip the blocker's fingers and fly straight back out of bounds. The blocker's touch might not count as one of the three hits, but it's certainly included in the "who touched it last" accounting.

The other hit is the wipe-off, a hit aimed right at the blocker's hands. The idea is to bring the ball back into your court, in a more controlled way, for three more hits. It's used when the set wasn't very good, and an attack might fail. A wipe-off can also be used when the ball is near the sidelines. The ball can be hit against the blocker's hands at such an angle that it bounces over the sideline. This is tough to do, however.

Teaming Up for a Block

If the kill wasn't quite mortal enough, then the ball is going to come right back at the team. This time, however, it won't be from a serve, so there are two new factors to consider. First, the players are already in their appropriate spots, with the starting positions long since abandoned. Second, the attack can be blocked. The blocker and one other player next to her try to move where they think the attack is going to come from. They jump up at the last minute and try to get their hands on the ball. The double block is effective because it covers more area.

FOUL TIME

Volleyball is a physically demanding sport, but since the two teams are kept apart by a net, there isn't any physical contact to deal with. Nonetheless, the referee has more to do than just make line calls.

When a player hits a ball, it must be a clean hit. It can't be lifted or carried at all. A *lift* looks almost like the player is pushing the ball rather than hitting it. A ball also can't be *double hit,* which happens when the two hands don't connect with the ball at exactly the same time.

The ball may be touched only by the arms and hands. If the ball is touched by any other part of the body, the play is a foul.

GAMES PEOPLE PLAY

Obviously, competitive volleyball is considerably different from the volleyball many people remember from picnics, gym class, and backyards, but that doesn't mean the casual kind of volleyball can't be played.

Here are some other games that you and your children and friends can play in the backyard.

Nameball

The great thing about *Nameball* is that you don't need a net. A ball, a wide-open area, and at least three players will do just fine.

Players stand in a fairly large circle. One player tosses the ball up into the middle of the circle and calls out the name of another player. That person must go into the circle, set the ball up again, and call out someone else's name. (The balls should be hit straight up, not to a particular person.)

If a player makes a bad set or misses a set with her name on it, then she gets a point. The first one to 10 points loses, and the player with the fewest points at that time is the winner.

Beach Volleyball

As a first guess, you'd probably think that *beach volleyball* is the same as picnic volleyball, except that you play in bare feet in the sand. Well, you need to go to door number 2.

Beach volleyball is an official sport that's televised, has tournaments, and even qualifies for the Olympics. The game is played with just four people, two to a side. Games are still played to 15 points, but the players switch sides after every five points.

There are still three hits to a side, but the block now counts as one of the hits. To compensate for that rule change, the blocker can be the one to take the second hit. In other words, even if she just touched it for the block, she can hit it again.

Other than that, the game is basically the same. With only two players on a side, however, it's an incredible workout.

Crosscourt

Crosscourt is a game that requires a large playing area and many people. It can be played with as few as eight players, but the more the better. It's a good outdoor party game.

There are four nets, each with a common center pole. Players divide into four equal teams and set up in each of the courts created by the four nets. There are two balls.

Two teams next to each other serve simultaneously to their diagonal court. The players on that court then send the ball to any other court. Points are negative and are given when the ball touches the ground, is hit out of bounds, or fails to be sent to another court within three touches. When a team reaches 15 points, it leaves the court. The remaining teams play until there's only one left: the winner.

Once a point has been given, the team making the error puts the ball back into play. The players on that team can choose to hold it out until both balls are dead, if they want.

LEARNING THE LINGO

There's a lot more to volleyball than you originally thought, so saying "Hit it over the net" doesn't quite cut it anymore. The following table lists the terms every volleyball mom should know to sound a little more savvy about the game.

Volleyball lingo	
TERM	*EXPLANATION*
attack area	The area 10 feet out from the center line. Only players starting in that area when the ball is served may attack or block from that area.

continues

Volleyball lingo *continued*

TERM	EXPLANATION
blocker	The player whose primary role on the team is to block the attack from the other team. The blocker stands in the middle front of the court.
digging	Receiving the ball after an attack.
double hit	Hitting the ball first with one hand, then the other.
forearm pass	The way most players receive the serve. It sends the ball up to the setter spot.
high flat	A hard shot parallel to the floor, intended to catch the tips of the blocker's fingers.
lift	Carrying the ball or pushing it into the air rather than hitting it.
opposite	The player who stands opposite the setter in the rotation.
rotating	Moving positions after each side out.
serving box	The 10-foot area at the endline where the serve must come from.
set	A soft, set-up shot for the attack.
setter	The player running the show for the team, determining where the attack is coming from.
setter spot	The place that the setter moves to, close to the net and off to one side, after the serve.
siding out	When the team that's not serving wins the rally.
spike	The kill shot—a shot that's directed toward the floor.

TERM	EXPLANATION
swing hitter	The player on the team who digs most of the attacks and hits some of the spikes.
wipe-off	A hit directly into the blocker's hands with the purpose of either bringing it back into the court or out of bounds.

Volleyball is a fast-paced, complicated game. The team must develop perfect timing to get off a good kill shot or block a spike from the other team. The players have to be in great shape; moms just have to sit back and watch an exciting game.

THE LEAST YOU NEED TO KNOW

◆ Volleyball is played between two teams of six on a volleyball court.

◆ Games are played to 15, and only the serving team can score a point. The nonserving team just wins the opportunity to serve.

◆ Even though the players rotate positions on the court, each player is assigned a specific job to do on both offense and defense.

Wrestle with This

When your toddler rolled on the living room floor with his uncle, you thought it was cute. When he was a six-year-old hellion tackling his younger sister, you strained your vocal chords yelling. At ten, he wore you down, and the phrase, "Boys, stop wrestling," changed into, "Boys, take that outside, please." When will this ever end? you wondered. And then, last week, he told you he won a coveted spot on the wrestling team. You're not only supposed to sanction this sport, but you're also supposed to cheer him on.

Well, cheer on and cheer up. Wrestling is an ancient and revered sport. The athletes who do it need to be flexible, strong, and in top condition. Good wrestlers are highly skilled and learn intricate moves that can help them out of any tight spot. That can certainly come in handy for a teenager, don't you think?

This chapter covers the rules and guidelines that govern a wrestling match. It describes some of the moves your child will be making and the points he'll be getting for his team. It also alerts you to some of the health dangers associated with the sport. Finally, it wraps up with a lesson in lingo.

> ### BET YOU DIDN'T KNOW
>
> There are two types of wrestling: freestyle wrestling and Greco-Roman wrestling. Freestyle wrestling is the form most high schools use (with some added restrictions), and it's the earliest form of wrestling, founded on the philosophy that anything goes. Cave men probably did freestyle wrestling.
>
> Greco-Roman wrestling came later. In this style of wrestling, no part of the legs can be used. (Obviously, his legs can support the wrestler, but he can't use them to take someone out, and he can't grab onto his opponent's legs.) As a result, in Greco-Roman wrestling, you see a lot of lifts in the air, meaning the wrestler is lifted and then thrown down on the mat. Ouch!

ON THE MAT

The wrestling mat is a 32-square-foot mat (or one that's 32 feet in diameter if it's round). In high school, a wrestling match lasts three *periods*, and each one is two minutes long.

Wrestlers wear a *singlet*, which is a one-piece sleeveless unitard, with the legs cut as shorts or pants. They also wear special wrestling shoes, which are light and have no heels. In the past decade, wrestling headgear has been introduced to protect the ears.

The two wrestlers who face each other are generally about the same weight. It would hardly be fair for your 250-pound behemoth to wrestle against the classic 98-pound weakling (as gratifying as it might be in the match). Wrestlers are put into *classes* depending on how much they weigh. (Can you just imagine suggesting this idea to high school girls? That must be the reason you don't see girl wrestlers.) If your son is wrestling in the 167-pound weight class, you know that everyone he wrestles with will be 167 pounds or slightly less.

There are thirteen weight classes at the high school level:

- 98 pounds
- 105 pounds
- 112 pounds
- 119 pounds
- 126 pounds
- 132 pounds
- 138 pounds
- 145 pounds
- 155 pounds
- 167 pounds
- 185 pounds
- 210 pounds
- Heavyweight (more than 210 pounds)

Ideally, a team would like to get wrestlers in every weight class, but that's not always possible. If the other team has a wrestler in a weight class that you don't, you have to forfeit that particular class.

INSTANT REPLAY

The prestigious Lawrenceville School once had a heavy wrestler who was close to being over the 210-pound cutoff. He desperately wanted to get in under the cutoff, but wasn't sure he would. Just before stepping on the scale, he stripped off his singlet and got on buck naked. It worked—he just barely qualified.

STARTING POSITIONS

In the first period, the wrestlers stand up and face each other. Of course, the "facing each other" part seems a bit unnecessary to state. I mean, really, if someone was going to try to tackle you, throw you to the ground, and pin your shoulders to the mat, would you turn your back?

The second and third periods begin a little differently. For the second period, the referee flips a special wrestling coin. The coin has a different color on each side, matching the team colors. The team member whose color comes up gets to choose which spot he will take in the *referee's position*.

The two spots in the referee's position are called the *top* and *bottom* positions. The wrestler on the bottom is on his hands and knees. The wrestler in the top position is on one knee, to the side of the bottom person. He has one hand on the bottom person's arm near the elbow and the other arm over the back with the hand around the bottom person's stomach.

Of course, any mom who sees her child in the bottom position is going to think it's terribly unfair to give the other wrestler that great advantage, but that's not really the case. If your child is good at a move called a *reversal* (which I'll explain later on), he can quickly get out of this situation and get a lot of points at the same time. Besides, when the next period starts, the positions are reversed.

The match ends when one person is pinned (described in the following section) or when the clock runs out.

ON PINS AND POINTS

A pin for a win. It's every wrestler's dream, but it's not always that easy. To *pin* an opponent, a wrestler must get both of his opponent's shoulders to touch the mat at the same time and hold that position for at least two seconds. If that happens, the match is immediately over.

Even though the pin, also called a *fall*, is the ultimate goal of a wrestling match, it doesn't always work out that way if the two opponents are evenly matched. Competitive wrestling has a point system for certain common moves. If wrestlers can execute the moves successfully, they earn the allotted points. Then, when time runs out and no one has been pinned, the wrestler with the most points is the winner.

Here are the main point scorers:

◆ **takedown**   Bringing the opponent down to the mat from a neutral position (that is, neither wrestler has an advantage). It's worth two points.

◆ **reversal**   When one wrestler is at a disadvantage and immediately turns it around (see the section "Reversals" later in this chapter) so that the other player is at a disadvantage. It's worth two points.

◆ **escape**   Getting away from the opponent and a disadvantaged position and into a neutral position. It gets a mere one point.

◆ **nearfall**   When a wrestler almost pins his opponent but doesn't quite. It earns two or three points, depending on how long the other wrestler is on his back.

BET YOU DIDN'T KNOW

A player who is really in control in a nearfall position can rack up some points. He can get the points for a long nearfall, roll his opponent onto his side, and then roll him back onto his back for another nearfall. As long as he can keep doing this, he can get nearfall points. However, there's a good chance that if someone has this much control over an opponent, he'll be able to get a pin before long.

MAKING A MOVE

Wrestling isn't just a free-for-all, with the two wrestlers grappling without direction. There are specific moves wrestlers learn that help them get closer to a pin. There are also some moves they learn to avoid because they're illegal.

The Step of Champions

The first move your child should learn is called the *Step of Champions*. It's basically learning how to take a hit (if your wrestler has older siblings, I'm sure he's already familiar with this one).

If a wrestler can't maintain his balance when an opponent comes after him, all his other moves are worthless. This is where the Step of Champions comes in. If your son has learned it, you will see him shoot his right leg forward and drop his chest when an opponent comes toward him. This counterbalances the attacker's blow and keeps the center of gravity low and over your son's feet.

The Step is pretty basic and instinctual. If your son is stepping backward instead, he might want to find a new sport.

Takedowns

When the match begins, the two wrestlers are facing each other. Each one desperately wants to get the other down on the mat, which is called a *takedown*. There are several popular ways to perform one.

The *single-leg takedown* is one of the simplest. The wrestler goes down on one knee, grabs his opponent's leg, and then quickly stands back up while still holding onto the leg. In addition, the wrestler should also be pushing his head against his opponent's hip. If all this works correctly, the opponent's one-legged, off-balance, head-butted body should topple.

The *double-leg takedown* is similar, but a little harder to do. The wrestler goes down on one knee, as before, but places his knee between the other guy's legs. Next, the wrestler grabs both of his opponent's legs and stands up as before.

Reversals

A reversal happens when a player at a disadvantage is able to put himself at an advantage. Your child will have to be very quick to be good at reversals. He needs to dislodge the player hanging on to his back and get him over onto *his* back. The two most popular techniques for reversals happen from the second and third period starting positions; they are the *sit-and-spin* and the *tuck-and-roll*.

For the sit-and-spin, the wrestler grabs the hand that's on his stomach, sits down on the hip on that side (in other words, moving away from the opponent), and leans into the arm that's over his back. If he can spin around quickly, the opponent will end up on his back.

The tuck-and-roll is similar. The wrestler should grab the hand on his stomach again and roll away, bringing the opponent with him, over and onto his back. When doing a tuck-and-roll, however, he should remember two crucial points. First, tuck his elbows in tight to his body. Elbows sticking out all over the place don't make for a smooth or quick roll. Second, hold on tight. If the wrestler lets go, then he's pretty much given away a pin. He'll be rolling onto his back while the other guy is still in the top position. Not much of a reversal, huh?

Lock It Up

Several moves don't necessarily earn points, but are still important enough to qualify for official names:

◆ **tie-up**   Essentially a neutral position. The two wrestlers are standing, but locked together, both trying to get a good grip somewhere, but nothing is really happening.

◆ **headlock**   A very effective way to immobilize an opponent. It might also be called, in Mom-ese, a stranglehold. The wrestler is behind the opponent with one arm around his neck. This hold must also go through the armpit to be legal.

◆ **hiplock**   Happens when a wrestler has grabbed across his opponent's body at the hip level. If he has a good grip at the hips, it's an easy throw.

These moves might not get points, but they certainly help win the match.

All the Wrong Moves

Here are some illegal moves that might give an opponent some points or end up disqualifying the wrestler who made them:

◆ Throwing the opponent to the mat

◆ Grabbing the opponent's clothing

◆ Leaving the mat

◆ Stalling, such as trying to avoid wrestling

◆ Holds over the mouth, nose, eyes, or throat

◆ Any strangleholds

◆ Any forcing of a joint in the wrong direction

◆ Pulling on fewer than four fingers at once

◆ A *full nelson*, which is a hold from the back with both arms under the armpits and the hands behind the neck

◆ A headlock without an arm included

If a player uses any of these holds, he will give a point to the opponent. After three of them, the wrestler is disqualified. Players can also be disqualified for unsportsmanlike behavior, using greasy stuff on their skin, or an illegal uniform.

TO GOOD HEALTH

As a mom, you might be worried about some of the health risks involved with wrestling. Stories of cauliflower ear, wrestling herpes, and pronounced weight loss abound. The truth is that all of them can be prevented. Keep an eye on your child and make sure his school's program doesn't sacrifice a wrestler's health for the sake of a win. Because of all the restrictions, wrestling is actually one of the safest sports your child can be involved in.

Weight Watchers

Wrestling has gotten a bad reputation because of the weight loss issue. Its detractors haven't quite reached the frenzied pitch they've reserved for gymnastics and ballet, but they have brought wrestling weight-loss issues to the country's attention.

They do have a point. It's not healthy for a young person to starve or dehydrate himself just to fit into a certain weight class. Each wrestler should accept his weight and wrestle in that class. Most coaches and programs are aware of this safeguard, but monitor your child to make sure he doesn't get out of control.

Here are some tips to help your son keep a healthy attitude toward weight and wrestling:

◆ Make sure your son eats his meals. You probably can't do much about lunch, but you can watch breakfast and dinner.

◆ Watch the clothes he wears when he goes for a run. Some young wrestlers wear three sweatsuits and a hat while jogging indoors and don't drink any water in an effort to sweat out some extra water weight. This is a recipe for passing out rather than losing weight.

◆ Talk to the coach if you think he might be pressuring your son. It could be that the school has a glut of kids in your son's weight class, and the coach is encouraging him to lose a little to fill an empty slot.

Wrestlers are weighed right before the match, but after they have been weighed, they can do what they want before they actually wrestle. From the second they step off the scale, you'll see most of the kids inhaling large hoagies, Power Bars, candy, and so forth to get energy while they're guzzling Gatorade and Big Gulps to replenish fluids.

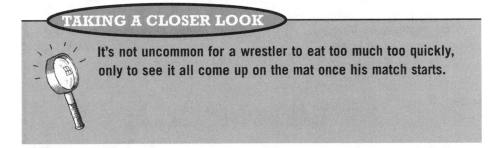

TAKING A CLOSER LOOK

It's not uncommon for a wrestler to eat too much too quickly, only to see it all come up on the mat once his match starts.

Cauliflower Ear

Cauliflower ear used to be very common in wrestling. Because of constant abuse, wrestlers' ears would accumulate extra blood in the tissues. This created a very unsightly, lumpy look, hence the name. The use of headgear has pretty much eliminated this problem.

I don't know about you, but I've often thought I've gotten cauliflower ear after an hour on the phone.

Skin Stories

Skin diseases, such as *wrestling herpes* (which is a contagious skin disease), are occasionally a problem because wrestlers can often get *mat burn* when their skin is rubbed against the mat. This abrasion creates an opening for germs to enter.

To guard against this problem, any wrestler with a skin disease is completely barred from the wrestling mat. Most schools are good about enforcing this, and most referees will catch a problem if the school hasn't stopped it.

All the mats should be cleaned with a disinfectant and detergent after each match. (You might want to check to make sure your son's school does this.)

> **INSTANT REPLAY**
>
> In a recent wrestling scandal, an undefeated team was having an incredible season when the players found out that one of their teammates had wrestling herpes. Even though the teammates barred the wrestler from the mat, they were afraid that other schools would back out of matches if they found out. Their season would be over, so they kept on playing until a newspaper broke the story.

LEARNING THE LINGO

As your child is wrestling on the mat, you'll be grappling with the sport's rules and regulations. The following table helps you learn the terms.

Wrestling lingo	
TERM	*EXPLANATION*
bottom position	A position taken at the start of the second or third period. The wrestler in the bottom position is on his hands and knees.

TERM	EXPLANATION
escape	Getting away from the opponent, out of a disadvantaged position, and into a neutral position.
fall	Another term for a pin.
full nelson	An illegal hold from the back with both arms under the armpits and the hands behind the neck.
headlock	Holding on to the opponent from behind with one arm around his neck.
hiplock	Holding on to an opponent across his hips.
nearfall	When a wrestler almost pins his opponent, but doesn't quite accomplish it.
neutral position	When a wrestler has neither the advantage nor the disadvantage. Two wrestlers standing across from each other is an example of a neutral position.
pin	When one wrestler has forced both of the other wrestler's shoulders to the mat and held them there for at least two seconds.
referee's position	The position the two players take at the beginning of the second and third periods.
reversal	When one wrestler is at a disadvantage and immediately turns it around so that the other player is at a disadvantage.
singlet	The one-piece uniform that a wrestler wears.
Step of Champions	Shooting the right leg forward and dropping the chest to the mat to maintain balance when under attack.
takedown	Bringing the opponent down to the mat from a neutral position.

continues

Wrestling lingo *continued*	

TERM	EXPLANATION
tie-up	When both wrestlers are locked together, but neither is gaining an advantage.
top position	A position taken at the start of the second or third period. The wrestler in the top position is on one knee, with one hand near the opponent's elbow and the other arm over the opponent's back, with the hand on the opponent's stomach.

Wrestling has evolved dramatically from caveman days. The rules and restrictions governing the sport make it very safe, hardly combat at all. It might pain you to watch your son getting thrown on his back, but he's probably not hurting much. Relax and enjoy the sport. The better he gets, the more likely it will be that he's doing the throwing.

THE LEAST YOU NEED TO KNOW

◆ A wrestling match consists of two teams putting their members against each other, one on one, in an effort to get a pin.

◆ Wrestlers are given points for different moves they make, so they can still win a round even if they haven't gotten a pin.

◆ Many wrestling moves are considered unsafe, so they are banned from the sport.

◆ The danger in wrestling comes from the wrestler who might try to manipulate his body to make a certain weight class.

Moms: The Ultimate Fans

You managed to get the kids signed up for their sports (and getting to the Y at 6:00 a.m. for those soccer signups was a real killer), you've read up on the rules (you had to learn practically a whole new game of volleyball), and now you're all ready to be a fan, right? Wrong.

There's a whole lot left to being a sports mom. You have to feed your little athletes a healthy diet, you have to make sure your child stays healthy on the field, you have to make constant repairs to scraped knees and bruised egos, and, most important, you have to know how to be a good fan. This chapter covers all that.

BLEACHER BEHAVIOR

When pressed, most parents come up with similar reasons for signing their children up for sports:

◆ Sports teach teamwork.

◆ Sports build confidence.

◆ Sports help you learn to deal with competition.

◆ Sports help you learn to win and lose gracefully.

◆ Sports are good for the health.

◆ Kids love to play sports.

◆ Sports are fun.

But when the kids are out on the field or the court or the ice or the course, you'd never know the benefits of sports. In fact, judging from the comments of some parents, it seems like they're teaching something entirely different:

◆ Teamwork: "Don't pass it off, Johnny! Take the shot yourself!" or (my favorite) "Coach, get her out of there. She's making them lose!"

◆ Confidence: "How did you ever miss that easy ground ball?!"

◆ Competition: "It wasn't your fault. They were dirty players…and it was raining…and the field was bad and…."

◆ Win and lose gracefully: "Ref, are you blind?!!"

◆ Healthy: "Don't be a wimp. Get back in there and play."

◆ Fun: "Even if you think it's boring now, you'll appreciate learning tennis when you're older."

If you (or your husband or friends) have made some of these comments, try to remember why you're there in the first place. Pay attention to what you're yelling from the stands. When Tyler, the neighbor kid who just happens to be playing for the enemy, gets up to bat, give him a cheer. "Go, Tyler!" Your child might later ask why you're cheering for the other team, but you'll have an easy answer that you can be proud of. "He's a friend of ours, and we like it when good things happen to our friends. Don't worry. I cheered for your team, too."

Now picture the scene another way. If, instead, you yell for the pitcher to strike Tyler out, you'll have quite a different scene later. Your child might ask why you were so mean to Tyler, and you'd have to say, "I wanted your team to win." Which message do you really want your child to get?

Basically, when you're in the bleachers, there are three rules to follow:

◆ Stay seated. No kid wants to hear someone say "Who's that crazy mom standing up and yelling at the ref?" and then see it's her mom doing the yelling.

◆ Support all kids. Even if you can't bring yourself to cheer for the other team's players, be sure to cheer for all the kids on your child's team, not just the stars. In fact, the less athletic kids need cheering the most.

◆ Pay attention. You don't want to miss your daughter's only goal of the season because you were exchanging recipes for barbecued Vidalia onions in the bleachers. I guarantee you that your child is looking to the bleachers the second after she scores, and she'll know whether you saw it.

INSTANT REPLAY

One of the worst instances of fan interference in the history of sports came in 1982, during a football game between the Stanford Cardinals and the Berkeley Weenies. The game had been close the whole way; with five seconds left in the game, a field goal put Stanford up by two. The Stanford fans went wild. There were only two seconds left, so they were basically guaranteed a win. Stanford did a short kick-off, so the team could be on top of the Berkeley player when he caught the ball. It looked like the plan went beautifully. The player went down, the band started marching onto the field, and the fans poured out of their seats. But the Berkeley player had thrown a lateral pass back to another player, and he in turn did another lateral pass. In the confusion, the Weenies managed to get the ball down the field for a touchdown. The game was over. Berkeley had won. The thousands of celebrating Cardinal fans down on the field had only themselves to blame.

OUCH!

Your child goes down screaming. You fly off the bleachers, adrenaline pumping, as you race toward her at the speed of light. "She stepped on my toe!" wails your little hypochondriac. Another false alarm.

Or maybe not. After she sits out five minutes, you see that she's still in pain. Now what? you ask. Now it's doctor time. If your child is injured, don't assume it will go away. It can get worse if it's not treated or allowed to heal.

It's especially important to be vigilant with overuse injuries, which you might not catch because they aren't caused by a specific incident. If your child is complaining of pain somewhere, however, it probably means something. Kids rarely fake an injury. In fact, usually the opposite is true. Kids love to play and sometimes ignore the pain cues their bodies are sending.

INSTANT REPLAY

I remember a nine-year-old soccer player named Jamie who was the star of the team and couldn't wait to get on the field. At one game, she took a tumble and went down in obvious pain. The game stopped, and the parents, coaches, and refs took a look at her. She calmed down and said she felt okay to play. They took her word for it and she played the last 10 minutes of the game, looking fine. Coming off the field, however, she started limping, and then hopping. The pain was clearly getting worse. Her parents took her straight to the doctor. Sure enough, she had a serious injury: a hairline fracture in her shin bone! Her desire to play was so strong that she suppressed the pain until the end of the game.

If you suspect your child is trying to hide an injury so she can play, watch her body language. If she's limping or rubbing her shoulder or something along those lines, then she needs to rest. Don't let an injured child play. An injury that might have taken only a week to heal (remember, kids heal quickly) might end up needing surgery if the damage continues.

A QUICK FIRST-AID LESSON

One way you can help your child is to take a first-aid course. Often the coach isn't certified in first aid (especially if the coach is just another parent in the community), so your knowledge can really make a difference in those first crucial moments after a serious injury. I can't give you an entire first-aid course; but here are some basic tips every mom should know.

RICE

The treatment for sprains, strains, and bruises can be remembered by a simple acronym: RICE. It can speed up healing considerably.

- ◆ **R for Rest**   Make your child stay off the injury as much as possible. If it's in his legs, try to get some crutches. If it's in his arm, put it in a sling. If he uses the injured area, he's not allowing his body to repair itself.

- ◆ **I for Ice**   The minute an injury occurs, apply ice to the area. The accumulation of blood in the area causes painful swelling, but ice will shrink the blood vessels to minimize the amount of swelling. The less swelling, the less time it takes for the injured area to return to normal. Keep applying ice as often as possible for at least two days.

- ◆ **C for Compression**   Wrap the injured area with an Ace bandage or something similar. Compression works with ice to keep the swelling down.

- ◆ **E for Elevation**   This measure allows the blood that has already reached the injured part to drain away from the injury. Try to raise the injured part above the heart, which could mean the child lying down and putting his sprained ankle up on a pillow, for instance.

Just remember: The more swelling, the more pain. So anything you do to minimize the amount of blood that rushes to the injury, the more comfortable your child will be and the faster he will heal.

A Real Head-Banger

A blow to the head should always be treated as a serious injury, even though there's a good chance it's not. The problem with head injuries is that they can be extremely dangerous, even though symptoms aren't immediately apparent. A second blow to the head, right after the first, could conceivably be fatal.

Here are some signs of a concussion:

◆ Vomiting or nausea

◆ One eye dilating more than the other one

◆ Unsteady walk

◆ Incoherent talk or amnesia

◆ Numbness

◆ Dizziness

◆ Seeing stars or hearing bells

◆ Unconsciousness

If you see any of these signs, take your child to the doctor for a real diagnosis. This is not a wait-and-see type of injury.

Back or Neck Injuries

If you suspect that your child has a neck or back injury because you saw the injury happen or because she is complaining of pain in those areas or numbness in her legs, do *not* move her under any circumstances!

If she's conscious, you can ask her to try to get up herself. If she can do that, you don't have to worry. But if she's unconscious or unable to stand up, get an ambulance to the site immediately. Her neck needs to be stabilized, but this isn't something an untrained parent can do. Get the professionals on the job.

Hot Enough For You?

Children can be prone to *heat exhaustion* or *heat stroke*. They are serious problems, so parents and coaches need to be aware of them.

Heat exhaustion is caused by dehydration. The child usually feels dizzy and tired and should rest in a shady area and drink lots of fluids.

Heat stroke is very serious. The child typically turns beet-red, runs a fever, and possibly acts irrationally. This child needs his body cooled down immediately with ice or water and should be taken to the hospital.

A Few Other Boo-boos

So it's RICE for sprains, strains, and bruises. It's medical help for broken bones, concussions, and back and neck injuries. But what about the rest? Here's a quick rundown:

◆ Cuts: Bandage them up. If you can stop the bleeding, the child can go back in the game.

◆ Teeth: If a tooth is knocked out, it's emergency room time. Find the tooth and drop it in milk, salt water, or saliva. Do not use regular water or try to clean the tooth.

◆ Shortness of breath: Remove the child from the game until she can breathe normally again. If it was caused by a blow to the chest, she should see a doctor because blood might be collecting in her lungs. If you find this happening to your child a lot, you might want to ask your doctor about exercise-induced asthma. It's very treatable, but many children have quit sports because they just can't handle the exertion, without ever knowing they have a treatable type of asthma.

An Ounce of Prevention...

More important than treating the injury is preventing it before it happens. Here are some guidelines:

◆ Make sure the coach has your child's entire team stretch and warm up before they get into any strenuous activity.

◆ Make sure water is available and that the coach gives the kids lots of water breaks. If the program doesn't provide a big water keg, then make sure your child comes with his own.

◆ Make sure the program is suited to your child's age, size, and ability.

◆ Make sure the program supplies appropriate safety equipment, such as batting helmets, goalie pads, and so forth.

ALL ROADS LEAD TO HOME

If you're beginning to suspect that sports are going to invade your whole life, you're right. Once you have a budding athlete at home, you have a whole new set of variables to throw into the equation.

The Athlete's Diet

Kids playing sports need to be extra mindful of what they eat. What do you think the chances are that they will be? Not good, so you need to step in. Carbohydrates (like pasta, cereal, and bread) are the best food options for athletes because they supply long-term energy.

Short-term energy boosters, such as foods made with sugar and caffeine, are the worst. Your child is going to eat them before the match, get a boost on his way to the match or during warm-ups, and then crash just as he's about to play—not the best time to feel your body lose energy.

Some sports require extra attention when it comes to diet. Wrestling and gymnastics are the obvious examples as far as starvation problems go, but football has its own problems because many players (particularly linemen) try to bulk up by eating junk food or even using steroids. You have to impress upon your children the value of a healthy diet.

A healthy eater is a healthy athlete. A body deprived of vitamins is going to fall apart. Muscles need protein, bones need calcium, and blood needs iron. Weight training and exercise are much healthier ways to get the same effects. If you suspect steroid use or starvation, consult your doctor immediately.

Fit First

For your child to get the most out of sports, he needs to be fit and well rested. A tired child might not be picking his feet up as much as he should be, which could easily result in a fall. His concentration won't be sharp either, which can result in an injury. It's your responsibility to protect your child, and making sure he gets plenty of sleep is the first step in meeting that responsibility.

You want your child to be in good shape before he plays a sport. An overweight child has weaker joints because they weren't designed to carry the extra weight. It might seem as though getting your overweight child into a soccer program is the perfect cure for a weight problem, but it's not going to help at all if he ends up on the couch for four weeks, nursing a sprained knee back to health.

For the overweight child, you're better off managing his diet and starting some other form of exercise first. Swimming is an excellent choice because the water's buoyancy takes the weight off his joints. Long family walks do a lot to reduce weight, too. Then, when your child has gotten most of the weight off, sports programs can work wonders maintaining his new, healthier body.

A Bruised Ego

One of the downsides of sports is the bench-sitting syndrome. A kid, excited at the start of the season, gradually becomes more and more discouraged as games go by and she doesn't get to play. What can you do?

Depending on the level of play, you have a few options. If it's a school team, you can say something to the coach, but schools generally give the win-loss record more importance than the equal-playing-time-for-all-kids philosophy. With a town recreation league, though, speaking to the coach should help. He might not realize he has been neglecting your daughter so much.

If a talk doesn't work, then suffer through until the end of the season and do what you can to get your child on another coach's team the next time around. Rec leagues are designed so that everyone can play. Most coaches are pretty good about getting all the kids in the game for a certain chunk of time.

Chances are, however, that if your child is sitting out more than the others, she is probably not up to their athletic level. This is something your child needs to understand. Mommy can't just step in and tell the coach to play her more because the object of the game is, after all, to win.

You can tell your child, however, that you'll practice more with her so she can improve her skill level. This encouragement and practice will do a whole lot more for her playing time than a talk with a coach. If she's really committed to the sport, you can even suggest a specialty camp in the summer.

Above all, don't let your child quit just because she isn't getting playing time. Teaching her that she made a commitment and must stick with it is important. But if she's truly miserable and doesn't want to make the time commitment to improve, then you should definitely let her stop at the end of the season. There's no need to keep signing her up for misery.

BET YOU DIDN'T KNOW

The National Basketball Association has a player named Muggsy Bogues. He's the shortest player in the history of the sport—in fact, he's 5′3″! Yet he was determined to make it to the pros despite this obvious basketball handicap. He worked hard, never gave up, and achieved his dream. Just a little story for you to pass on to your junior quitter.

Remember, you can always have your child try a new sport. There's something out there for everyone. There are 10 sports discussed in this book and a whole bunch of others I didn't even cover. The joys, health benefits, and life lessons a child can get from sports are well worth the effort to find the perfect fit.

THE LEAST YOU NEED TO KNOW

◆ Try to be supportive and positive in the bleachers.

◆ Pay attention to what's going on in the game.

◆ Follow good first-aid guidelines.

◆ Make sure your little athlete has a healthy and fit mind and body.

Glossary

50-yard line (football) The line dividing the field in half.

ace (tennis) A serve that completely blows by the opponent.

ad court (tennis) The left side of the court.

ad in (tennis) When the server is ahead by one. This can occur only after the players have already reached deuce.

ad out (tennis) When the receiver is ahead by one. This can occur only after the players have already reached deuce.

advantage (soccer) When a referee allows a foul to occur without penalty, so the offensive team won't lose its advantage over the defensive team.

advantage (tennis) When one person is leading by one point after at least seven points have been played.

alley (tennis) The sides of the court, which are used only in doubles.

apron (golf) The area of slightly longer grass surrounding the green.

at bat (baseball) A turn up at the plate.

attack area (volleyball) The area 10 feet out from the center line. Only players starting in that area when the ball is served may attack or block from that area.

attacking zone (ice hockey) The area between the opponent's blue line and goal line.

backboard (basketball) The board behind the basket.

backcourt (basketball) The defensive side of a court. Obviously, it's different for each team.

backhand court (tennis) The left side of the court.

balk (baseball) When a pitcher stops his pitching motion without delivering the pitch.

ball (baseball) A pitch that's not over the plate or between the batter's knees and shoulders.

ball   A spherical object used in many sports. It comes in different sizes and shapes.

base (baseball)   One of the four corners of the diamond where a batter is safe from being tagged by the ball.

base path (baseball)   The dirt area between the bases.

basket (lacrosse)   The net part of the lacrosse stick.

batter (baseball)   The player trying to hit the pitch.

batting average (baseball)   The number of at bats a player has had, divided by the number of successful hits.

blocker (volleyball)   The player whose primary role on the team is to block the attack from the other team. The blocker stands in the middle front of the court and teams up with another player to make a wall.

boards (ice hockey)   The four-foot-high wall around the rink.

body-checking (ice hockey)   Throwing the hip or shoulder into another skater.

body-checking (lacrosse)   Hitting the opponent with the body (only legal in boys' lacrosse).

bottom position (wrestling)   A position taken at the start of the second or third period. The wrestler in the bottom position is on his hands and knees.

boxing out (basketball)   Putting your body in a position that keeps the other team from getting the rebound.

breaking a serve (tennis)   When someone beats her opponent when the opponent is the one serving.

bunker (golf)   A sand trap.

bunt (baseball)   A hit in which the batter spreads his hands on the bat and pushes the bat toward the ball rather than swinging at it.

caddie (golf)   The person who carries a player's clubs around the course, often offering advice.

casual water (golf)   Water that isn't supposed to be on the course, so is therefore not a water hazard. You may pick your ball up and take a free drop near it, no closer to the hole.

catcher (baseball)   The position behind the plate.

center (basketball)   Usually the tallest player on the team. Stands near the basket on both offense and defense.

center (football)   The lineman who snaps the ball.

center (lacrosse)   The midfielder who takes the face-off (boys' lacrosse) or the draw (girls' lacrosse).

checking (lacrosse)   Hitting an opponent's stick.

clear (ice hockey)   Sending the puck away from the goal.

clear (soccer)   When the defensive team kicks the ball far away from the defensive area, stopping the offensive drive to the goal.

completion (football)   A pass that makes it from the quarterback to the receiver without hitting the ground.

conversion (football)   The extra point or points that can be earned after a touchdown.

cornerback (football)   A defensive back who usually tries to cover the receivers.

cover point (lacrosse)   The middle defense player in girls' lacrosse.

cradling (lacrosse)   Carrying the ball in the stick while running. The technique uses a rapid rocking motion to keep the ball in the pocket by centrifugal force. It can be a two-handed or one-handed motion.

crease (ice hockey)   The area around the goal where only the goalie is allowed to be.

crease (lacrosse)   The circle around the goal where only the goalie is allowed to play.

cross (soccer)   A pass from one side of the field to either in front of the goal or the other side of the field.

crosse (lacrosse)   The lacrosse stick.

cup (golf)   The actual hole.

defending zone (ice hockey)   The area between a player's goal line and the first blue line.

defense   When a team or a group of players is trying to prevent the other team from scoring.

defensive back (football)   The defensive players who are the farthest back from the line.

deuce (tennis)   When the score is tied at three or more points each.

deuce court (tennis)   The right side of the court.

diamond (baseball)   The infield.

dig (volleyball)   Receiving the ball after an attack.

divot (golf)   A chunk of grass removed by the club during a shot. It should be replaced.

double dribble (basketball)   Dribbling, stopping, and then trying to dribble again in the same possession.

double fault (tennis)   Two missed serves in a row, resulting in a lost point.

double hit (volleyball)   Hitting the ball first with one hand, and then the other.

double play (baseball)   When a team gets two outs during one turn at bat.

doubles (tennis)   When two players play against two other players.

down (football)   A try or play. Teams are allowed four of them in each possession.

draw (lacrosse)   The beginning of the girls' game; two players hold their sticks up in the air and trap the ball between the backs of the basket.

dribble (soccer)   The way a player keeps the ball in her possession and moves it down the field. It's usually done on the ground with light taps from the feet.

dribbling (basketball)   Bouncing the ball one-handed.

drive (golf)   The first shot off the tee.

drop shot (tennis)   A short shot with a lot of spin that barely makes it over the net. Used mostly when the other player is way back at the baseline.

dugout (baseball)   The bench area where a team sits when it's not in the field.

end (football)   A defensive line man.

end line (football)   The ends of the field, 10 yards beyond each goal line.

end zone (football)   The area between the goal line and the end line where a touchdown is scored.

ERA (baseball)   Earned run average.

escape (wrestling)   Getting away from the opponent, out of a disadvantaged position, and into a neutral position.

face (lacrosse)   Another term for *face-off*.

face-off (ice hockey)   The way the puck is put back in play.

face-off (lacrosse)   The beginning of the boys' game; two players hold their sticks on the ground, trapping the ball between the backs of the basket.

fair ball (baseball)   A ball hit within the foul lines.

fair catch (football)   When a player signals he won't run a kick back so he can avoid being tackled.

fairway (golf)   The groomed area leading up to the green.

fall (wrestling)   Another term for a *pin*.

fast break (basketball)   Racing down the floor and taking the ball to the hoop ahead of the defense.

fault (tennis)   A missed serve.

field goal (football)   When the ball is kicked through the goalposts on the fourth down. It's worth three points.

first baseman (baseball)   The player covering the area around first base.

first home (lacrosse)   The frontmost attacker in girls' lacrosse.

fly ball (baseball)   A ball hit into the air in the outfield.

force play (baseball)   When a player must run to the next base. In this case, only the base needs to be tagged (not the runner) to make an out.

"Fore!" (golf)   What golfers yell if the ball is heading toward another golfer.

forearm pass (volleyball)   The way most players receive the serve. It sends the ball up to the setter spot.

forehand court (tennis)   The right side of the court.

forward (basketball)   The position for the taller players on the team, usually playing on each side of the basket.

forwards (soccer)   Primarily offensive players. They begin the kick-off on the center line.

foul   A rules infraction (except in baseball).

foul ball (baseball)   A ball hit outside the foul lines.

foul line (basketball)   The line at the top of the key where the foul shots are taken.

foul lines (baseball)   The lines that lead from home plate past first and third bases and into the outfield.

foul shot (basketball)   A free shot given to a player after a foul.

free position (lacrosse)   Restarting play after a foul has occurred; the fouled player gets possession of the ball, and everyone is cleared at least five yards away.

free throw (basketball)   Another term for foul shot.

full nelson (wrestling)   An illegal hold from the back with both arms under the armpits and the hands behind the neck.

fullback (football)   A player who runs with the ball.

fullbacks (soccer)   Primarily defensive players. They begin the kick-off nearest to the goalkeeper.

fumble (football)   When a player drops the ball.

glove (baseball)   The leather device worn on the hand to help the fielder catch the ball.

goal   The place where points are scored.

goal area (lacrosse)   The area in boys' lacrosse where the attack players must remain during the face-off.

goal line (football)   The zero-yard lines on each end of the field.

goalkeeper (lacrosse)   The player protecting the goal and the only player allowed in the crease.

goalkeeper (soccer)   The person who stands in the goal, wears a different color shirt, and is allowed to use his or her hands.

goalkeeper, goaltender   The player who guards the goal.

goalposts (football)   The two upright posts on the end line through which the ball must pass during a conversion or a field goal.

green (golf)   The finely mowed area around the hole. Only putting is allowed on the green.

grounder (baseball)   A ball hit along the ground.

guard (basketball)   The position for the smaller, quicker players.

guard (football)   An offensive lineman.

half-volley (soccer)   Occurs when a player kicks the ball at exactly the same time that it touches the ground.

halfback (football)   An offensive player who runs the ball.

halfbacks (soccer)   Also called midfielders. These players are the link between the fullbacks and the forwards. They are responsible for offense and defense and cover the whole field.

hat trick (ice hockey)   One player scoring three goals in one game.

hat trick (soccer)   Three goals scored in one game by a single player.

hazard (golf)   A water trap or sand trap.

heading (soccer)   Hitting the ball with the forehead to make a pass or a shot on goal.

headlock (wrestling)   Holding on to the opponent from behind with one arm around his neck.

high flat (volleyball)   A hard shot parallel to the floor, intended to catch the tips of the blocker's fingers.

hiplock (wrestling)   Holding on to an opponent across his hips.

hole (golf)   One "unit" in golf, from the tee box to the green.

home (baseball)   The plate.

home plate (baseball)   A rubber pentagon that determines where the pitch must be thrown.

home run (baseball)   A hit that allows the player to go all the way around the bases in one turn without getting an out.

honors (golf)   Winning the previous hole.

hook (golf)   A shot that curves to the left (for a right-handed golfer).

huddle (football)   When the team meets to plan a play.

icing (ice hockey)   Shooting the puck from behind the center line over the opponent's goal line.

inbounding (basketball)   A pass that puts the ball back onto the court after the ball has gone out of bounds or after a shot has been made.

infield (baseball)   The area outlined by the bases and base paths.

infield fly rule (baseball)   A rule that says if a ball is hit in the air in the infield with runners on base and less than two outs, then it's an automatic out for the batter whether or not the ball is caught.

inning (baseball)   A unit of play consisting of six outs, three by each team. A baseball game consists of nine innings. A softball game consists of seven.

interception (football)   When the defense catches a pass.

irons (golf)   Metal clubs with a flat blade on the end.

jump ball (basketball)   The way the game begins. The ball is tossed in the air between two players who try to tap it to teammates.

key (basketball)   A six-foot wide area between the foul line and the base line.

kick-off (football)   The start of play at the beginning of a half or after a score.

lay-up (basketball)   A close shot, usually done on the run.

left attack wing (lacrosse)   One of the side players in girls' lacrosse.

left defense wing (lacrosse)   One of the side players in girls' lacrosse.

let (tennis)   A do-over.

lift (volleyball)   Carrying the ball or pushing it into the air rather than hitting it.

line of scrimmage (football)   The place where the ball is put at the start of the play. Neither team may cross this line until the ball is snapped.

linebacker (football)   The middle line of defense.

lob (tennis)   A high shot used when the other player has rushed the net. It gets the ball over his head and forces him back.

love (tennis)   The score of zero.

mark up   To guard or cover a player.

marking (soccer)   Guarding an opponent.

match play (golf)   A game in which the holes won, rather than thc strokes, are counted.

mitt (baseball)   Another name for a glove.

mixed doubles (tennis)   When a male and female team play against another male and female team.

mulligan (golf)   A do-over, usually off the first tee. It's illegal, but a common practice during friendly matches.

nearfall (wrestling)   When a wrestler almost pins his opponent but doesn't quite.

neutral position (wrestling)   When a wrestler has neither the advantage nor the disadvantage. Two wrestlers standing across from each other is an example of a neutral position.

nutmeg (soccer)   Dribbling the ball between the defensive player's legs.

offside (ice hockey)   When an attacking player is ahead of the puck in the attacking zone.

one-and-one (basketball)   A foul shot; the player gets a second free throw if the first one goes in.

onside kick (football)   A kick on the kick-off that goes slightly more than 10 yards.

opposite (volleyball)   The player who stands opposite the setter in the rotation.

out (baseball)   When the fielders stop the batter or runner from reaching a base.

outfield (baseball)   The grassy area beyond the infield.

outfielder (baseball)   One of three players covering the outfield.

pass   The transfer of the ball (or puck) from one player to another player on the same team.

passing (basketball)   Throwing the ball to another teammate.

passing (soccer)   Kicking the ball among players of the same team.

pin (wrestling)   When one wrestler has forced both of the other wrestler's shoulders to the mat and held them there for at least two seconds.

pitch (baseball)   The throw to the batter.

pitcher (baseball)   The player who throws the ball to the batter.

pitcher's mound (baseball)   The area where the pitcher stands when she delivers the pitch.

pivot foot (basketball)   The foot that remains in one spot while the rest of the body moves. A player needs a pivot foot only when she has the ball and is not dribbling it.

place kicker (football)   The player who kicks the ball for a field goal or kick-off or conversion.

point (lacrosse)   The defensive player in girls' lacrosse who is closest to the goalkeeper.

point guard (basketball)   The ball handler of the team.

poke-checking (lacrosse)   Jabbing at a player with the stick (legal only in boys' lacrosse).

pop-up (baseball)   A short fly ball.

possession arrow (basketball)   The arrow that shows which team gets the ball when two players are both holding on to it.

power play (ice hockey)

pro   A person who's paid to play the sport.

punter (football)   The player who kicks the ball on the fourth down.

putter (golf)   The club used to tap the ball into the hole when you're on the green.

rally (tennis)   A series of hits.

RBI (baseball)   An abbreviation for runs batted in.

rebounding (basketball)   Retrieving the ball after a missed shot.

referee   The official who makes sure that all the rules are followed. See also *umpire*.

referee's position   The position the two players take at the beginning of the second and third periods.

reversal (wrestling)   When one wrestler is at a disadvantage and immediately turns it around so that the other player is at a disadvantage.

right attack wing (lacrosse)   One of the side players in girls' lacrosse.

right defense wing (lacrosse)   One of the side players in girls' lacrosse.

rotating (volleyball)   Moving positions after each side out.

rough (golf)   The ungroomed area around the fairway.

run (baseball)   The unit of scoring in baseball. Occurs when a player has tagged all three bases and home plate safely.

running back (football)   A player who runs with the ball.

sack (football)   When the quarterback is tackled behind the line of scrimmage.

sacrifice fly (baseball)   Hitting the ball in the air to the outfield so that a runner may tag up and score.

safety (football/position)   The last line of defense.

safety (football/score)   When a team is tackled in its opponent's end zone. Worth two points to the defensive team.

second baseman (baseball)   The fielder covering the area between second and first.

second home (lacrosse)   The second attacker in girls' lacrosse.

service box (tennis)   The area that the serve must bounce into.

serving box (volleyball)   The 10-foot area at the endline where the serve must come from.

set (volleyball)   A soft, set-up shot for the attack.

setter (volleyball)   The player running the show for the team, determining where the attack is coming from.

setter spot (volleyball)   The place that the setter moves to, close to the net and off to one side, after the serve.

shoot   An attempt to score.

shooting (basketball)   Throwing the ball toward or into the basket.

shooting (soccer)   Kicking the ball with the intention of scoring.

short fielder (baseball)   The tenth player in slow-pitch softball. She is positioned behind second base.

shortstop (baseball)   The fielder covering the area between third and second base.

siding out (volleyball)   When a team that's not serving wins the rally.

singles (tennis)   When one player plays one other player.

singlet (wrestling)   The one-piece uniform that a wrestler wears.

slice (golf)   A shot that curves to the right (for a right-handed golfer).

slide tackle (soccer)   Stealing the ball from an opponent by sliding into it on the ground. The sliding player must touch the ball first or it will be a foul.

snap (football)   When the center hands the ball to the quarterback.

special teams (football)   The group of people who take the field during a kick.

spike (volleyball)   The kill shot.

stealing (baseball)   Running to the next base at some time other than after a hit.

Step of Champions (wrestling)   Shooting the right leg forward and dropping the chest to the mat to maintain balance when under attack.

stopper (soccer)   The frontmost defensive player.

strike (baseball)   A good pitch that was swung at but not hit.

strike out (baseball)   To miss three good pitches during an at bat.

sweeper (soccer)   The last defensive player.

swing hitter (volleyball)   The player on the team who digs most of the attacks and hits some of the spikes.

T-ball (baseball)   The first kind of baseball most kids play; the ball is propped up on a tee instead of being pitched.

tackle (football)   An offensive or defensive line player.

tackle (soccer)   Stealing the ball away from another player.

tag up (baseball)   Waiting until a fly ball is caught and then trying to run to the next base or home before the throw gets there.

takedown (wrestling)   Bringing the opponent down to the mat from a neutral position.

team   A group of players all working together to win a game.

tee (golf)   A small wooden device that props up the ball.

tee box (golf)   The area at the start of the hole.

third baseman (baseball)   The fielder guarding the area near third base.

third home (lacrosse)   The attacker third in line in girls' lacrosse, closest to the midfield.

third man (lacrosse)   The defensive player in girls' lacrosse who is closest to the center.

throw (lacrosse)   When the ref in girls' lacrosse restarts the ball by tossing it between two players.

throw-in (soccer)   Inbounding the ball when it has been kicked over the sideline.

tie-up (wrestling)   When both wrestlers are locked together but neither is gaining an advantage.

tight end (football)   An offensive player who can run, pass, or block.

top position (wrestling)   A position taken at the start of the second or third period. The wrestler in top position is on one knee, with one hand near the opponent's elbow and the other arm over the opponent's back, with the hand on the opponent's stomach.

touch (soccer)   Contact with the ball. In a *two-touch pass*, a player receives it with one motion and then uses a second motion to pass the ball to a teammate. A *one-touch pass* means that the player received the ball and passed it, all in one motion and with only one moment of contact with the ball.

touchdown (football)   Crossing the goal line with the ball. Worth six points.

trapping (soccer)   Taking control of the ball, especially when the ball is coming out of the air.

traveling (basketball)   Moving both feet while in possession of the ball without dribbling the ball.

triple play (baseball)   When a team gets three outs during one at bat.

umpire (baseball)   The official running the game.

volley (soccer)   Kicking the ball when it is in the air.

volley (tennis)   A shot out of the air, where the ball doesn't bounce on the court.

walk (baseball)   When a batter receives four unacceptable pitches from the pitcher. He gets to go to first base.

wall (soccer)   A defensive structure, usually four players wide, in front of the goal. It is set up when the opponents are taking a direct kick and must be at least 10 yards from the ball.

wide receiver (football)   An offensive player who is the primary target for a pass.

wing area (lacrosse)   The portion of the field where the side midfielders must remain until the ref blows the whistle for the face-off.

wings (soccer)   The players positioned on the sides of the field. They can be forwards, halfbacks, or fullbacks.

wipe-off (volleyball)   A hit directly into the blocker's hands with the purpose of either bringing it back into the court or out of bounds.

woods (golf)   The clubs, no longer made of wood, that have a block on the end. They are used for long shots.

Resources

If you want more information about a particular sport, here are some addresses and phone numbers of organizations that can answer your questions:

BASEBALL
Little League Baseball
P.O. Box 3485
Williamsport, PA 17701
(717) 326-1921

BASKETBALL
Amateur Athletic Union
P.O. Box 10000
Lake Buena Vista, FL 32830-1000
(800) AAU-4USA

FOOTBALL
Amateur Athletic Union
P.O. Box 10000
Lake Buena Vista, FL 32830-1000
(800) AAU-4USA

GOLF
American Junior Golf Association
2415 Steeplechase Lane
Roswell, GA 30076
(770) 998-4653

ICE HOCKEY
USA Hockey
1775 Bob Johnson Drive
Colorado Springs, CO 80906
(719) 599-5500

LACROSSE
The Lacrosse Foundation
Newton H. White Athletic Center
Baltimore, MD 21218
(410) 235-6882

SOCCER
U.S. Soccer Federation
1801-1811 S. Prairie Avenue
Chicago, IL 60616
(312) 808-1300

TENNIS
U.S. Tennis Association
70 West Red Oak Lane
White Plains, NY 10604
(914) 696-7000

VOLLEYBALL
Amateur Athletic Union
P.O. Box 10000
Lake Buena Vista, FL 32830-1000
(800) AAU-4USA

WRESTLING
USA Wrestling
6155 Lehman Drive
Colorado Springs, CO 80918
(719) 598-8181

Index

G

R

rackets (tennis)
  grip, 61
  head, 61
  throat, 61
recreational sports leagues
  cost and fees, 7
  safety factors, 7
  signups, 7
  time commitment, 7
RICE (Rest, Ice, Compression and
    Elevation), 153
"running the bases" (baseball), 46

S

sand traps (golf), 77
school sports programs
  equipment, 7
  junior varsity, 7
  varsity, 7
selecting sports, criteria, 2-3
slow pitch softball, 52
soccer
  4-2-2 formation, 20
  4-3-3 formation, 19
  backyard variations, 20
    juggling, 21
    Pass for Points, 20
    Ten and Again, 21
  center line, 12-13
  corner kicks, 16
  differences with American football, 12
  direct kicks, 15
  drop kicks, 16
  equipment, 13
  field diagram, 12-13
  goal kicks, 13, 16
    wall formations, 17
  indirect kicks, 15
  kickoff, 12-13
  Major League Soccer, 11
  number of players, 14
  object of game, 14
  offsides, 17-18
  penalty kicks, 13-15

players
  fullbacks, 19
  goalie, 19
  halfbacks, 19
  midfielders, 19
  strikers, 19
  sweeper, 19
  wing fullbacks, 19
  wing halfbacks, 19
referees
  red cards, 15
  yellow cards, 15
role of sweeper, 18-19
rules, 12-14, 17-19
six-yard line, 13
sportsmanship, 15
terminology, 22-23
throw-ins, 17
time length, 14
typical play, 14
use of hands, 14
wall formations, 17
softball
  fast pitch, 53
  slow pitch, 52
sports
  ability factor, 3
  bench-sitting syndrome, 157-158
  benefits, 1-2
  economic costs, 5-6
  fan behavior
    coaches, 8-9
    parents, 8-9
  glossary, 159-171
  importance of child's fitness, 157
  injuries
    hidden, 152
    treating, 152
  injury potential, 4-5
  interest factor, 3
  nutrition guidelines, 156
  objectives, 150-151
  organizations
    information, 173-174
    resources, 173-174
  parental behavior at events, 150-151
  playing through pain, 152

W - Z

Game-time Guides from *Mom's Guide to Sports*. Available in retail stores everywhere!

Created by Vicki Poretta from the *Mom's Guide* series, game-time reference guides serve as a quick and handy way to learn all about the rules, strategies and basic terms of sports. Twelve sport guides in the series!

For more information, visit us on the web at **www.momsguide.com**

Mom's Guide to Sports Game-time Guides are published by Big World Media, Inc. Boston, MA.